Editor
Erica N. Russikoff, M.A.

Contributing Editor
Karen McRae

Illustrators
Mark Mason
Renée Christine Yates

Cover Artist
Tony Carrillo

Editor in Chief
Ina Massler Levin, M.A.

Creative Director
Karen J. Goldfluss, M.S. Ed.

Imaging
Rosa C. See

Publisher

Mary D. Smith, M.S. Ed.

Teacher Created Resources, Inc.
6421 Industry Way
Westminster, CA 92683
www.teachercreated.com
ISBN: 978-1-4206-8843-6

Table of Contents

Monday	Math:	*Patterned Out*
	Reading:	*Prefixes*
Tuesday	Math:	*Writing Numbers*
	Writing:	*Capitalization*
Wednesday	Math:	*Count the Dice*
	Reading:	*Sequencing Events*
Thursday	Math:	*Collecting Values*
	Writing:	*Alliteration*
Friday	Friday Fun:	*Solve This One, Find the Past Tense*

Monday	Math:	*This Is the Life!*
	Writing:	*What Did He Say?*
Tuesday	Math:	*Two-Digit Addition*
	Reading:	*Suffixes*
Wednesday	Math:	*Challenging Addition*
	Writing:	*Strong Verbs*
Thursday	Math:	*Can You Make 105?*
	Reading:	*Irrelevant Details*
Friday	Friday Fun:	*What's in the Box?, A Purple Ear*

Monday	Math:	*Coin Flip*
	Reading:	*Sneaky Snake*
Tuesday	Math:	*I've Been Framed!*
	Writing:	*What Do You Mean?*
Wednesday	Math:	*Two-Digit Subtraction*
	Reading:	*The Secret*
Thursday	Math:	*Subtract and Regroup*
	Writing:	*Acting Out Verbs*
Friday	Friday Fun:	*Smallest Number, Map Madness!*

Monday	Math:	*Counting Sets*
	Writing:	*Defining Descriptions*
Tuesday	Math:	*Multiplication Table*
	Reading:	*Compound Words*
Wednesday	Math:	*Twos and Threes*
	Writing:	*It's Crunchy!*
Thursday	Math:	*Mysterious Fives*
	Reading:	*On the Beach*
Friday	Friday Fun:	*Designer Shoes, Which Number Am I?*

Monday	Math:	*It's Easy to Divide!*
	Reading:	*Seeing and Hearing*
Tuesday	Math:	*Grouping*
	Writing:	*Lists*
Wednesday	Math:	*Find the Number*
	Reading:	*Movie Poster*

Table of Contents (cont.)

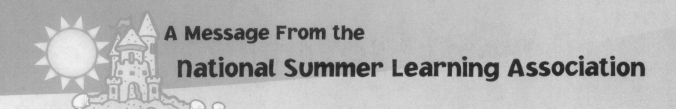

A Message From the
National Summer Learning Association

Dear Parents,

Did you know that all young people experience learning losses when they don't engage in educational activities during the summer? That means some of what they've spent time learning over the preceding school year evaporates during the summer months. However, summer learning loss *is* something that you can help prevent. Summer is the perfect time for fun and engaging activities that can help children maintain and grow their academic skills. Here are just a few:

- ☼ Read with your child every day. Visit your local library together, and select books on subjects that interest your child.

- ☼ Ask your child's teacher for recommendations of books for summer reading. The Summer Reading List in this publication is a good start.

- ☼ Explore parks, nature preserves, museums, and cultural centers.

- ☼ Consider every day as a day full of teachable moments. Measuring in recipes and reviewing maps before a car trip are ways to learn or reinforce a skill. Use the Learning Experiences in the back of this book for more ideas.

- ☼ Each day, set goals to accomplish. For example, do five math problems or read a chapter in a book.

- ☼ Encourage your child to complete the activities in books, such as *Summertime Learning*, to help bridge the summer learning gap.

Our vision is for every child to be safe, healthy, and engaged in learning during the summer. Learn more at *www.summerlearning.org* and *www.summerlearningcampaign.org*.

Have a *memorable* summer!

Ron Fairchild
Chief Executive Officer
National Summer Learning Association

How to Use This Book

As a parent, you know that summertime is a time for fun and learning. So it is quite useful that fun and learning can go hand in hand when your child uses *Summertime Learning*.

There are many ways to use this book effectively with your child. We list three ideas on page 6. (See "Day by Day," "Pick and Choose," and "All of a Kind.") You may choose one way on one day, and, on another day, choose something else.

Book Organization

Summertime Learning is organized around an eight-week summer vacation period. For each weekday, there are two lessons. Each Monday through Thursday, there is a math lesson. Additionally, during the odd-numbered weeks, there is a reading lesson on Monday and Wednesday and a writing lesson on Tuesday and Thursday. During the even-numbered weeks, these lessons switch days. (Reading lessons are on Tuesday and Thursday, and writing lessons are on Monday and Wednesday.) Friday features two Friday Fun activities (one typically being a puzzle). The calendar looks like this:

Day	Week 1	Week 2	Week 3	Week 4	Week 5	Week 6	Week 7	Week 8
M	Math ---------- Reading	Math ---------- Writing	Math ---------- Reading	Math ---------- Writing	Math ---------- Reading	Math ---------- Writing	Math ---------- Reading	Math ---------- Writing
T	Math ---------- Writing	Math ---------- Reading	Math ---------- Writing	Math ---------- Reading	Math ---------- Writing	Math ---------- Reading	Math ---------- Writing	Math ---------- Reading
W	Math ---------- Reading	Math ---------- Writing	Math ---------- Reading	Math ---------- Writing	Math ---------- Reading	Math ---------- Writing	Math ---------- Reading	Math ---------- Writing
Th	Math ---------- Writing	Math ---------- Reading	Math ---------- Writing	Math ---------- Reading	Math ---------- Writing	Math ---------- Reading	Math ---------- Writing	Math ---------- Reading
F	Friday Fun ---------- Friday Fun	Friday Fun ---------- Friday Fun	Friday Fun ---------- Friday Fun	Friday Fun ---------- Friday Fun	Friday Fun ---------- Friday Fun	Friday Fun ---------- Friday Fun	Friday Fun ---------- Friday Fun	Friday Fun ---------- Friday Fun

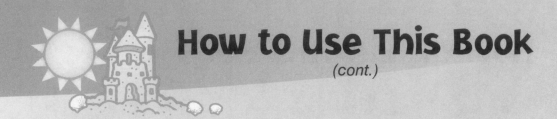
Day by Day

You can have your child do the activities in order, beginning on the first Monday of summer vacation. He or she can complete the two lessons provided for each day. It does not matter if math, reading, or writing is completed first. The pages are designed so that each day of the week's lessons are back to back. The book is also perforated. This gives you the option of tearing the pages out for your child to work on. If you opt to have your child tear out the pages, you might want to store the completed pages in a special folder or three-ring binder that your child decorates.

Pick and Choose

You may find that you do not want to have your child work strictly in order. Feel free to pick and choose any combination of pages based on your child's needs and interests.

All of a Kind

Perhaps your child needs more help in one area than another. You may opt to have him or her work only on math, reading, or writing.

Keeping Track

A Reward Chart is included on page 10 of this book, so you and your child can keep track of the activities that have been completed. This page is designed to be used with the stickers provided. Once your child has finished a page, have him or her put a sticker on the castle. If you don't want to use stickers for this, have your child color in a circle each time an activity is completed.

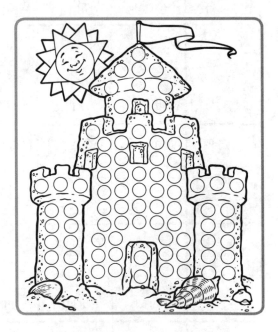

The stickers can also be used on the individual pages. As your child finishes a page, let him or her place a sticker in the sun at the top of the page. If he or she asks where to begin the next day, simply have him or her start on the page after the last sticker.

There are enough stickers to use for both the Reward Chart and the sun on each page. Plus, there are extra stickers for children to enjoy.

Standards and Skills

Each activity in *Summertime Learning* meets one or more of the following standards and skills*. The activities in this book are designed to help your child reinforce the skills learned during second grade, as well as introduce new skills that will be learned in third grade.

Language Arts Standards

- Uses the general skills and strategies of the writing process
- Uses the stylistic and rhetorical aspects of writing
- Uses grammatical and mechanical conventions in written compositions
- Uses the general skills and strategies of the reading process
- Uses reading skills and strategies to understand and interpret a variety of literary texts
- Uses reading skills and strategies to understand and interpret a variety of informational texts
- Uses listening and speaking strategies for different purposes

Mathematics Standards

- Uses a variety of strategies in the problem-solving process
- Understands and applies basic and advanced properties of the concepts of numbers
- Uses basic and advanced procedures while performing the processes of computation
- Understands and applies basic and advanced properties of the concepts of measurement
- Understands and applies basic and advanced properties of the concepts of geometry
- Understands and applies basic and advanced concepts of statistics and data analysis

Writing Skills

- Evaluates own and others' writing
- Uses strategies to write for a variety of purposes
- Writes expository compositions
- Writes narrative accounts, such as poems and stories
- Writes autobiographical compositions
- Writes expressive compositions
- Writes in response to literature
- Uses descriptive language that clarifies and enhances ideas
- Uses paragraph form in writing
- Uses a variety of sentence structures in writing
- Uses pronouns in written compositions
- Uses nouns in written compositions
- Uses verbs in written compositions
- Uses adjectives in written compositions
- Uses adverbs in written compositions

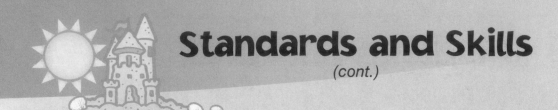

Standards and Skills

(cont.)

Writing Skills *(cont.)*

- ☼ Uses coordinating conjunctions in written compositions
- ☼ Uses conventions of spelling in written compositions
- ☼ Uses conventions of capitalization in written compositions
- ☼ Uses conventions of punctuation in written compositions

Reading Skills

- ☼ Previews text
- ☼ Establishes a purpose for reading
- ☼ Makes, confirms, and revises simple predictions about what will be found in a text
- ☼ Uses phonetic and structural analysis techniques, syntactic structure, and semantic context to decode unknown words
- ☼ Uses a variety of context clues to decode unknown words
- ☼ Uses word reference materials to determine the meaning, pronunciation, and derivations of unknown words
- ☼ Understands level-appropriate reading vocabulary
- ☼ Monitors own reading strategies and makes modifications as needed
- ☼ Adjusts speed of reading to suit purpose and difficulty of the material
- ☼ Understands the author's purpose or point of view
- ☼ Uses personal criteria to select reading material
- ☼ Uses reading skills and strategies to understand a variety of literary passages and texts
- ☼ Understands the basic concept of plot
- ☼ Understands the ways in which language is used in literary texts
- ☼ Makes connections between characters or simple events in a literary work and people or events in his or her own life

Mathematics Skills

- ☼ Uses a variety of strategies to understand problem situations
- ☼ Represents problem situations in a variety of forms
- ☼ Understands that some ways of representing a problem are more helpful than others
- ☼ Uses trial and error and the process of elimination to solve problems
- ☼ Knows the difference between pertinent and irrelevant information when solving problems
- ☼ Understands the basic language of logic in mathematical situations
- ☼ Uses explanations of the methods and reasoning behind the problem solution to determine reasonableness of and to verify results with respect to the original problem
- ☼ Understands basic number-theory concepts
- ☼ Understands equivalent forms of basic percents, fractions, and decimals and when one form of a number might be more useful than another

Mathematics Skills *(cont.)*

- ✿ Understands the basic difference between odd and even numbers
- ✿ Understands the basic meaning of place value
- ✿ Understands the relative magnitude and relationships among whole numbers, fractions, decimals, and mixed numbers
- ✿ Uses models to identify, order, and compare numbers
- ✿ Multiplies and divides whole numbers
- ✿ Adds, subtracts, multiplies, and divides decimals
- ✿ Adds and subtracts simple fractions
- ✿ Uses specific strategies to estimate computations and to check the reasonableness of computational results
- ✿ Performs basic mental computations
- ✿ Determines the effects of addition, subtraction, multiplication, and division on size and order of numbers
- ✿ Understands the properties of and the relationships among addition, subtraction, multiplication, and division
- ✿ Solves real-world problems involving number operations
- ✿ Knows the language of basic operations
- ✿ Selects and uses appropriate tools for given measurement situations
- ✿ Knows approximate size of basic standard units and relationships between them
- ✿ Uses specific strategies to estimate quantities and measurements
- ✿ Knows basic geometric language for describing and naming shapes
- ✿ Understands basic properties of figures
- ✿ Understands that shapes can be congruent or similar
- ✿ Understands characteristics of lines and angles
- ✿ Understands the basic concept of an equality relationship
- ✿ Solves simple open sentences involving operations on whole numbers
- ✿ Understands that numbers and the operations performed on them can be used to describe things in the real world and predict what might occur
- ✿ Understands that mathematical ideas and concepts can be represented concretely, graphically, and symbolically

* Standards and Skills used with permission from McREL (Copyright 2009, McREL. Midcontinent Research for Education and Learning. Address: 4601 DTC Boulevard, Suite 500, Denver, CO 80237. Telephone: 303-337-0990. Web site: www.mcrel.org/standards-benchmarks)

Reward Chart

Patterned Out

Directions: Fill in the missing numbers in the blank squares. Next, read the directions below, and color in the correct squares. When you are done, you will find a mystery word colored in your chart. Write the word at the bottom of the page.

0	1						7		
10			13						
20		22		24				28	
30				34		37			
40	41								49
50			53		55				
60	61							68	
70		72				76			
80					85				89
90						96			99

✿ Color the squares with a seven in the ones place.

✿ Color the squares with a one in the ones place.

✿ Color the squares with a three in the ones place.

✿ Color the squares that have more than 6 but less than 10.

✿ Color the squares that have more than 40 but less than 44.

✿ Color the squares that have more than 46 but less than 50.

✿ Color the squares that have more than 96 but less than 100.

✿ What is the hidden word? _____

Prefixes

Prefixes are letters added to the beginning of words to change their meanings. For example, "mis-" is the prefix of the word *misunderstood*.

Directions: Look at the meanings of the prefixes below. Then, write the meaning of each word on the line. The first two have been done for you.

☼ **dis-** = don't   ☼ **pre-** = before   ☼ **un-** = not

1. disobey _don't obey_

2. prejudge _judge before_

3. unhappy _____

4. disable _____

5. unlike _____

6. disagree _____

7. unbelievable _____

8. pretest _____

9. preschool _____

10. dislike _____

Writing Numbers

Directions: Write the numbers.

Example: one hundred sixty-nine __169_____

1. seven hundred seventy-eight _____

2. four hundred six _____

3. two hundred thirty-three _____

4. four hundred ninety-one _____

5. two hundred forty-seven _____

Directions: Write the following in expanded form.

Example: 868 __800__ + __60__ + __8__

6. 765 _____ + _____ + _____

7. 557 _____ + _____ + _____

8. 186 _____ + _____ + _____

9. 914 _____ + _____ + _____

10. 215 _____ + _____ + _____

Directions: Write the following using only words.

Example: 418 __four hundred eighteen_____

11. 129 _____

12. 365 _____

13. 790 _____

14. 661 _____

15. 296 _____

Capitalization

Capitalization Rule

Capitalize proper nouns, such as days, months, names, and titles of books and movies.

Directions: Circle the days, months, and titles you find in the sentences below. Then, rewrite each sentence using correct capitalization.

1. I had my birthday on a tuesday in december. _____

   _____

2. We will take a trip on a monday in june. _____

   _____

3. I saw a football game on a friday in october. _____

   _____

4. Our class went to see <u>the music man</u>. _____

   _____

5. We read <u>arrow to the sun</u> to study Native Americans. _____

   _____

6. My favorite book is <u>harry potter and the sorcerer's stone</u>. _____

   _____

Count the Dice

Math

Directions: Count the dots on the dice. Record the number and the written form. The first one has been done for you.

Dice	Number	Written Form
1.	341	three hundred forty-one
2.		
3.		
4.		
5.		
6.		
7.		
8.		

What was the smallest number made? _____

What was the largest number made? _____

Sequencing Events

Directions: Read the story. Then, write the events below in proper order.

On the night before her family vacation, Tracy began packing. She needed clothes that would keep her warm in the mountains. Tracy packed a coat and many warm sweaters. Then she packed some long pants, socks, and boots. Finally, Tracy packed some cozy pajamas. Just as she was ready to close her suitcase, she remembered her journal. She wanted to write about every detail of her vacation. As Tracy lay on her bed thinking of her exciting trip, she drifted off to sleep.

1. _____

2. _____

3. _____

4. _____

5. _____

☼ Tracy packed her socks.   ☼ Tracy packed her journal.

☼ Tracy fell asleep.   ☼ Tracy packed her coat.

☼ Tracy packed her pajamas.

Collecting Values

Directions: Look at the cans below. If the underlined digit is in the tens place, write the number in the tens-place barrel. If the underlined digit is in the hundreds place, write the number in the hundreds-place barrel. Place the ones in the ones-place barrel.

Alliteration

> **Alliteration** is the use of several words close together that begin with the same consonant.

Directions: Create alliterative sentences. Replace the underlined words with words from the Word Bank. Copy each new sentence on the line below it.

Word Bank

wind	berries	bear	snake	cried
silly	poured	two	breakfast	whipped
pavement	cushion	tiny	curled up	slithered

"c" words

1. The cat <u>sat</u> on the <u>pillow</u> and <u>meowed</u>.

_____

"s" words

2. One Saturday, a <u>funny</u> <u>reptile</u> <u>moved</u> in the dirt.

_____

"t" words

3. <u>A couple</u> <u>little</u> turtles walked to the city.

_____

"w" words

4. The cold <u>breeze</u> <u>blew</u> past the lake.

_____

"p" words

5. The rain <u>sprinkled</u> down on the <u>street</u>.

_____

"b" words

6. The <u>animal</u> ate <u>food</u> for <u>a meal</u>.

_____

Solve This One

Directions: Alice wants to stack boxes into the shape of a pyramid. If she starts with eight blocks on the bottom and stacks one less block on each layer, how many blocks will she use to complete the pyramid? Draw the blocks on top of each row to complete the pattern. Write the total number in the top block.

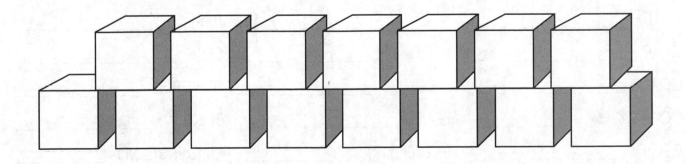

Find the Past Tense

Directions: The words below are in the present tense. Write them in the past tense on the lines, and then find them in the puzzle.

```
U  M  D  U  R  D  E  T  F  S  C  T  T
N  B  W  E  N  I  H  E  U  D  O  O  T
D  O  R  U  D  R  Z  R  F  W  O  F  U
E  U  O  E  E  I  P  W  E  T  K  M  V
R  F  K  W  C  R  C  N  D  S  E  T  Q
S  G  W  P  I  O  K  E  J  X  D  U  P
T  H  N  S  T  B  G  D  D  D  R  A  N
O  B  E  A  D  E  D  N  E  T  E  R  P
O  D  U  K  S  U  C  I  I  K  R  N  A
D  G  S  L  L  T  L  A  D  Z  S  G  V
H  C  L  A  P  P  E  D  U  R  E  A  N
E  V  U  Y  E  D  P  D  H  G  O  D  A
M  J  J  R  T  O  G  R  O  F  H  V  G
A  L  E  F  T  R  O  E  M  A  C  T  E
```

ASK _____

CATCH _____

CLAP _____

COME _____

COOK _____

DECIDE _____

DRIVE _____

FIND _____

FORGET _____

KNOW _____

LEAVE _____

PRETEND _____

RECOGNIZE _____

REPLY _____

SING _____

SURPRISE _____

THROW _____

UNDERSTAND _____

This Is the Life!

Directions: Solve each addition problem. Then, color the puzzle.

65 = green	**66** = brown	**67** = orange	**68** = yellow	**69** = blue

What Did He Say?

Punctuation Rules

Use quotation marks around a direct quote (words being spoken). Use a comma to set off a quotation within a sentence. Use a capital letter to begin each quotation.

Directions: Place a comma and quotation marks in each sentence below. The first one has been done for you.

1. Dr. Brown said, "You are as fit as a fiddle!"

2. Line up at the door said Mrs. Johnson.

3. Mom yelled Go, Cobras, go!

4. Sheila wondered Should I wear my blue dress?

5. My dad said You look nice today.

6. James asked May I have a glass of milk?

7. Please answer the phone whispered my mother.

8. Kelly exclaimed Look out!

9. My lizard escaped replied Henry sadly.

10. Juliette said I hope you can come over to play.

Two-Digit Addition

Example:

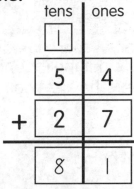

○ When adding two digits, always start on the ones side first.

○ Remember, there cannot be more than 9 ones on the ones side. So take 10 of the ones, and move that set of 10 to the tens side.

○ In the small square at the top of the left column (or tens column) record how many tens were moved to the tens side.

○ Now, put the remaining ones under the ones column. Add the tens, and write the number.

Directions: Complete the following addition problems.

1.

	tens	ones
	3	9
+	1	3

2.

	tens	ones
	4	2
+	2	8

3.

	tens	ones
	6	1
+	1	9

4.

	tens	ones
	2	5
+	2	5

5.

	tens	ones
	3	6
+	3	6

6.

	tens	ones
	1	8
+	1	7

Suffixes

> **Suffixes** are letters added to the end of words to form new words.
> For example, "-less" is the suffix of the word *sugarless*.

Directions: Use the two suffix meanings below to help you figure out the meaning of each word. Then, write the meaning of each word on the line. The first two have been done for you.

> ☼ **-ful** = having a lot of   ☼ **-ness** = a state of being

1. sadness _being sad_

2. delightful _having a lot of delight_

3. wonderful _____

4. careful _____

5. happiness _____

6. softness _____

7. colorful _____

8. joyful _____

9. loneliness _____

10. harmful _____

Challenging Addition

Directions: Write the answer to each addition problem. The first problem has been done for you.

1.

hundreds	tens	ones
1	1	
2	8	6
+ 1	2	9
4	1	5

2.

hundreds	tens	ones
2	9	7
+ 3	0	2

3.

hundreds	tens	ones
4	2	5
+ 1	3	8

4.

hundreds	tens	ones
5	0	7
+ 1	2	6

5.

hundreds	tens	ones
8	0	0
+ 1	0	3

6.

hundreds	tens	ones
7	2	7
+ 1	6	3

Strong Verbs

Directions: Write a verb on each line. Use the words in the Word Bank to help you.

Word Bank

| devoured | glanced | nibbled | stared | strolled |
| gazed | gobbled | paced | stomped | tiptoed |

1. The squirrel _____ on the nut.

2. The hungry lion _____ his food.

3. I got mad and _____ off.

4. When I _____ my dinner, my mom said to eat slowly.

5. She _____ over her shoulder and saw the boy chasing her.

6. He _____ at the math problem for a long time.

7. My dad _____ back and forth because he was worried.

8. The girl _____ at the handsome movie star.

9. I wanted to surprise my mom, so I _____ into the room.

10. The people _____ down the path.

Can You Make 105?

Directions: Arrange the numbers at the bottom of the page in the squares so that adding across in each row makes 105 and adding down in each column makes 105.

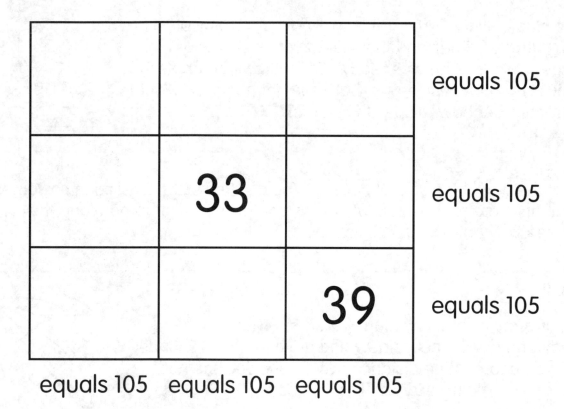

			equals 105
	33		equals 105
		39	equals 105

equals 105   equals 105   equals 105

31	32	34

35	36	37	38

Irrelevant Details

Directions: Read each paragraph. Find the sentence that does not fit with the rest of the sentences. Draw a line through it.

1. Katie studied very hard for the spelling test. She wrote each word ten times and then tried to spell each word without looking. She was ready! She wore a red dress to school. Then the test began, but Katie got nervous. Would she remember how to spell the words?

2. It was the day of the school parade. The children were dressed in costumes. The floats were ready to go. All of the parents were gathered along the sidewalks. I can't wait for Christmas.

3. The air grew cold as the storm rolled in. The sky was cloudy and dark. Shelly's new dog ate breakfast. Thunder could be heard in the distance. Shelly decided she had better take an umbrella with her to school.

4. Planting a flower garden is easy and fun. Daisies are pretty. All you need is a plot of dirt, some seeds, and water. First, you make several small holes in the dirt. Then, you sprinkle a few seeds in each hole and cover them with dirt. Just water the garden when it's dry, and in a few weeks, your garden will begin to grow!

5. Have you ever been to a circus? I love to see all of the animals do tricks. The elephants look smart, and the dancing bears are so cute. I love to watch the man on the trapeze. That looks scary. I wonder if I can go get pizza after the show.

What's in the Box?

Directions: Find the sums. Then, write the letter in each box that matches each sum. The first one has been done for you. Read the word you spell, and draw it in the box.

80	81	82	83	84	85	86	87
d	e	a	o	c	r	l	i

45 + 37 **82** [a]	17 + 67 [ ]	38 + 47 [ ]	58 + 25 [ ]	58 + 26 [ ]
36 + 47 [ ]	49 + 31 [ ]	69 + 18 [ ]	79 + 7 [ ]	48 + 33 [ ]

A Purple Ear

Directions: Fill in the Word Bank below, but do not look ahead at the story. Then, use the words from the Word Bank to complete your strange tale.

Word Bank

1. girl's name _____
2. animal _____
3. *-ing* action verb _____
4. girl's name from #1 _____
5. day _____

6. time you wake up _____
7. past tense verb _____
8. season _____
9. past tense verb _____
10. color _____

In a strange, mysterious jungle far, far away lived a small animal named

_____ . She was a(n) _____ . One of her friends,
　　　　1　　　　　　　　　　　　　　　　　2

Mary, had gone _____ in Rome. When she arrived home,
　　　　　　　　　　　3

_____ noticed that there was beautiful purple paint on Mary's left
　　　4

ear. She wanted her ear to look just like that, but no one sold purple paint in the

jungle. Every _____ at exactly _____ , she got up and
　　　　　　　　　5　　　　　　　　　　　　　　6

looked in the mirror with great sadness. Finally, Mary promised to bring home a can

of purple paint for her the next time she _____ to Rome.
　　　　　　　　　　　　　　　　　　　　　7

In the _____ , Mary _____ her bags and flew to Rome!
　　　　　8　　　　　　　　　　　9

You can guarantee she was at the airport when Mary came home. The purple paint

was in Mary's hand, but her ear was _____ now!
　　　　　　　　　　　　　　　　10

Coin Flip

Directions: First, find a penny. Then, flip the penny.

☼ Heads = The problem is solved using addition.

☼ Tails = The problem is solved using subtraction.

Continue flipping the coin and solving each of the problems in order. Write the sign on each problem. Good luck!

1. 780 132	2. 39 15	3. 932 407
4. 555 47	5. 312 88	6. 73 47
7. 2,804 97	8. 87 49	9. 643 554

Sneaky Snake

Directions: To find out what the sneaky snake has to say, solve the subtraction problems. Then, fill in the number code. When you are done, read the story.

15 – 10 = ____ **G**	17 – 6 = ____ **R**
20 – 19 = ____ **A**	13 – 6 = ____ **K**
20 – 8 = ____ **S**	14 – 11 = ____ **C**
17 – 15 = ____ **B**	17 – 9 = ____ **L**
20 – 11 = ____ **N**	12 – 6 = ____ **H**
16 – 12 = ____ **E**	13 – 3 = ____ **O**

What a sneaky snake I am! I get my name from my hard, turned-up

____ ____ ____ ____. If I think someone might harm me, I flatten
  9   10   12   4

my head and hiss. Then, I strike hard with my ____ ____ ____ ____ ,
                                 9   10   12   4

but I don't bite. If that doesn't work, I ____ ____ ____ ____ over and
                                11   10   8   8

play dead! If someone picks me up, I ____ ____ ____ ____ limply.
                            6   1   9   5

When I'm put back down, I flip over on my ____ ____ ____ ____ .
                                 2   1   3   7

I'm a ____ ____ ____ ____ ____ ____ ____ snake.
     6   10   5   9   10   12   4

I've Been Framed!

Math

Directions: Each number below is written within a different shape or frame. Using this as a guide, write the correct number in each shape below, and solve each problem. The first one has been done for you.

8	3	5
6	9	7
4	2	1

```
        49
   72        24
56       27       36
   32        64
        35
```

1. (35 – 5) + (27 – 3) = _____ 54 _____

2. (–) + (–) = _____

3. (–) + (–) = _____

4. (–) + (–) = _____

5. (–) + (–) = _____

What Do You Mean?

Directions: Determine two meanings of each word. Write two sentences using the word in different ways. The first one has been done for you.

1. **hide**

   Meaning #1: _The puppy likes to hide under the table._

   Meaning #2: _Leather is made from the hide of a cow._

2. **slip**

   Meaning #1: _____

   Meaning #2: _____

3. **fix**

   Meaning #1: _____

   Meaning #2: _____

Directions: Read each sentence, and circle the correct meaning of the underlined word.

4. Be sure to <u>post</u> your message on the bulletin board.

   ☼ a pole   ☼ put up

5. If I don't do a good job, the boss will <u>fire</u> me.

   ☼ flames   ☼ get rid of someone from work

6. Did you already <u>pack</u> for the trip?

   ☼ put clothes in a suitcase   ☼ wolves in a group

Two-Digit Subtraction

Directions: Complete the problems.

1.
tens	ones
2	0
– 1	0

2.
tens	ones
3	6
– 3	5

3.
tens	ones
3	9
– 2	7

4.
tens	ones
8	5
– 3	5

5.
tens	ones
7	8
– 4	8

6.
tens	ones
8	3
– 5	2

7.
8	0
– 1	0

8.
9	7
– 6	4

9.
7	8
– 1	5

10.
```
   2 5
 – 1 4
 _____
```

11.
```
   8 9
 – 4 1
 _____
```

12.
```
   9 1
 – 7 1
 _____
```

13.
```
   8 8
 – 2 8
 _____
```

14.
```
   9 4
 – 7 3
 _____
```

15.
```
   8 1
 – 6 1
 _____
```

The Secret

Directions: Read the story. Then, answer the questions.

Vanessa and Chloe woke up early on Saturday morning. "Mom is still asleep, I think," Vanessa whispered. "Maybe if we hurry, we can finish before she wakes up," replied Chloe. The girls tiptoed to the living room and pulled a large box from behind the couch. "Did you get the paper?" asked Vanessa. Chloe handed her the roll of bright red, yellow, and orange paper. "She's going to love this, don't you think?" Chloe smiled and said, "This will really help her in the garden." The girls finished wrapping the box and slid it behind the couch again. They heard some noises down the hallway and quickly jumped on the couch and pretended to be looking at books. "Girls," Mother said, "what are you up to?" "Nothing, Mom," they replied.

1. Who are Vanessa and Chloe? How do you know? _____

_____

2. Why were they whispering?_____

_____

3. What is special about this day?_____

_____

4. How do you think Mom feels about gardening? _____

_____

5. What do you think is inside the box? _____

_____

36

Subtract and Regroup

Example:

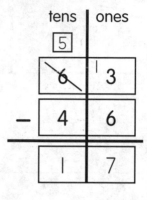

☼ In the problem 63 – 46, the 6 ones cannot be subtracted from the 3 ones. You will need to regroup.

☼ Take a ten from the 6 tens. Change the 6 tens to 5, and move the borrowed ten to the ones side. Add 10 to the 3 ones. Now, there are 5 tens and 13 ones.

☼ Subtract the 6 ones from the 13 ones. Write the answer.

☼ Subtract the 4 tens from the 5 tens. Write the answer.

Directions: Complete the following subtraction problems.

1.

tens	ones
8	6
– 1	7

2.

tens	ones
6	3
– 4	5

3.

tens	ones
9	0
– 5	5

4.

tens	ones
7	1
– 5	2

5.

tens	ones
5	3
– 2	8

6.

tens	ones
4	0
– 2	9

Acting Out Verbs

Directions: Look for the verbs, or action words, in each of the sentences below. Write the verb on the line. Then, act out the sentence.

1. The girl tripped over a tree branch. _____

2. The train rides down the track. _____

3. The monkey ate all the bananas. _____

4. The bear stood quietly in the road. _____

5. I scream during scary movies. _____

6. My teacher reads books. _____

7. The cat slept all day long. _____

8. Mark slipped on the banana peel. _____

9. The kids run a mile every day. _____

10. The coach jumped in the air. _____

Smallest number

Directions: Work your way through the maze. As you come to each choice, pick the path with the smallest number.

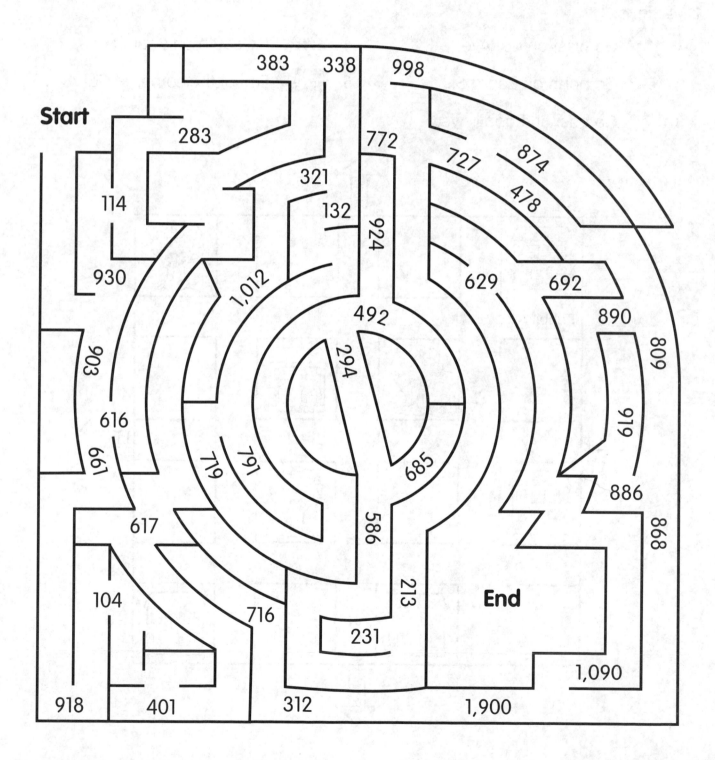

Map Madness!

Do you see Jan? She is lost! Follow the directions to get her back on track. Mark her ending spot with an **X**.

Directions:

1. ⬅ Go west on Cat Ave.

2. ⬆ Go north on Zebra St.

3. ➡ Go east on Rabbit Ave.

4. ⬇ Go south on Bear St.

5. **END** End at the corner of Cat Ave.

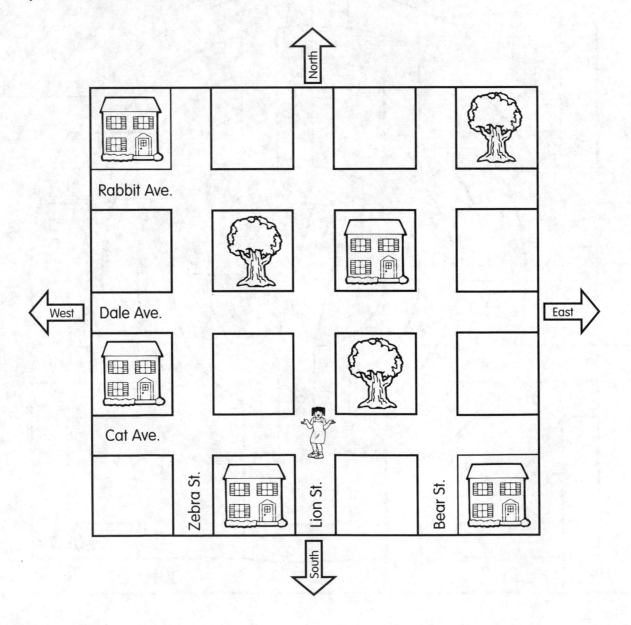

Counting Sets

Multiplication is a faster way to add sets with the same number of items.

Count and add the stars below (3 + 3 + 3 = 9 stars).

You can get the same number of stars by multiplying the number of sets times the number of items in each set (3 sets of stars x 3 stars in each set = 9 stars).

Directions: Count the number of sets and items in each set. Write the addition problem and the multiplication problem for each set of pictures.

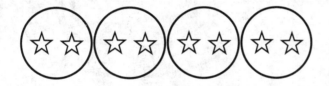

1. ____ + ____ + ____ + ____ = _____

2. _____ x _____ = _____
    (sets)   (items)   (product)

3. _____ + _____ = _____

4. _____ x _____ = _____
    (sets)   (items)   (product)

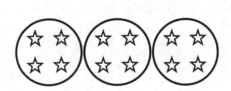

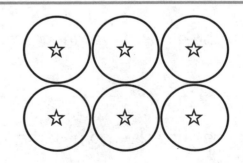

5. ____ + ____ + ____ = _____

6. _____ x _____ = _____
    (sets)   (items)   (product)

7. __ + __ + __ + __ + __ + __ = ____

8. _____ x _____ = _____
    (sets)   (items)   (product)

Defining Descriptions

> **Adjectives** are words that tell about, or describe, nouns.
> Adjectives make writing more interesting.

Directions: Circle the adjectives in each of the sentences below, and draw arrows to the nouns that the adjectives describe. The first one has been done for you.

1. The (chocolate) cake is finished.

2. The red licorice is all gone.

3. An angry man stormed out of the store.

4. Mrs. Jarski read us an interesting story.

5. David likes to write her long letters.

Directions: Fill in the blanks by thinking of your own adjectives.

6. List three adjectives that describe you.

_____   _____   _____

7. Write three adjectives that describe the kind of day you had.

_____   _____   _____

8. List three adjectives to describe your last family trip.

_____   _____   _____

9. Write three adjectives to describe your best friend.

_____   _____   _____

Multiplication Table

Directions: Complete the multiplication table by filling in the missing numbers.

X	0	1	2	3	4	5	6	7	8	9	10
0	0										0
1		1								9	
2		2	4		8				16		
3	0			9				21			
4					16		24				40
5						25	30	35	40	45	50
6					24		36	42	48	54	60
7	0			21	28		42	49	56	63	70
8			16				48	56	64	72	80
9		9					54	63	72	81	90
10	0						60	70	80	90	100

Compound Words

A **compound word** is made up of two or more words joined together.

Directions: Divide each compound word below into syllables using hyphens. The first one has been done for you.

1. football _____foot–ball_____

2. pigpen _____

3. snowshoe _____

4. playground _____

5. clipboard _____

6. shoelace _____

7. bedtime_____

8. nighttime _____

9. rainbow_____

10. sunshine _____

Twos and Threes

Directions: Complete each equation by writing the missing factor or product.

1. $2 \times 1 =$ _____

2. $2 \times 7 =$ _____

3. _____ $\times 3 = 9$

4. $2 \times$ _____ $= 2$

5. $2 \times$ _____ $= 16$

6. $3 \times 4 =$ _____

7. _____ $\times 3 = 6$

8. _____ $\times 9 = 18$

9. $3 \times$ _____ $= 15$

Directions: Answer each word problem.

10. Joanie has 2 marble bags. Inside each bag, there are 6 marbles. How many marbles does Joanie have in all? Joanie has _____ marbles in all.	11. Katie has 3 books. If she reads 10 pages in each book every day, how many pages does Katie read in a day? Katie reads _____ pages a day.
12. Each basket holds 2 apples. How many apples will the 8 baskets hold in all? The 8 baskets will hold ___ apples in all.	13. Mary has 3 dogs. Each dog can eat 5 dog treats a day. How many dog treats do Mary's dogs eat in a day? Mary's dogs eat _____ dog treats a day.

It's Crunchy!

Directions: Have you ever read a story that took you somewhere faraway? A good story uses the senses to make the reader feel like he or she is really there. Here's a challenge for you. Try writing one sentence for each of the five senses, according to the directions below. Write so that those who read your sentences will see, hear, smell, taste, or feel what you have described.

1. Write a sentence that shows what the ocean **looks** like. Do not use the words *big*, *huge*, or *blue*.

   _____

   _____

2. Write a sentence that shows what a cat's purr **sounds** like. Do not use the words *quiet* or *low*.

   _____

   _____

3. Write a sentence that shows how a flower **smells**. Do not use the words *pretty* or *good*.

   _____

   _____

4. Write a sentence that shows what chocolate **tastes** like. Do not use the words *creamy*, *good*, or *sweet*.

   _____

   _____

5. Write a sentence that shows how a snake **feels.** Do not use the words *slimy* or *slithery*.

   _____

   _____

Mysterious Fives

Directions: Solve each multiplication problem. Write the letter that goes with the answer for each problem on the line at the bottom of the page. What is the question?

5	10	15	20	25	30	35	40	45	50	55
A	C	I	L	M	N	O	P	T	U	Y

1.
$$2 \times 5$$

2.
$$5 \times 1$$

3.
$$6 \times 5$$

4.
$$5 \times 11$$

5.
$$5 \times 7$$

6.
$$10 \times 5$$

7.
$$5 \times 5$$

8.
$$5 \times 10$$

9.
$$5 \times 4$$

10.
$$5 \times 9$$

11.
$$3 \times 5$$

12.
$$8 \times 5$$

13.
$$4 \times 5$$

14.
$$11 \times 5$$

___ ___ ___ ___ ___ ___ ___ ___ ___ ___ ___ ___ ___ ___?
1   2   3   4   5   6   7   8   9   10 11 12 13 14

On the Beach

Directions: Read the story below, and then think about another way the story could have ended. What else could have happened? Write your new ending on the lines.

Carlos and Zoe often went to the beach. Carlos liked to pick up shells, and Zoe enjoyed watching the birds.

But one day, the children found something very different. Carlos saw it first because he was looking at the sand.

"Zoe," said Carlos, "Come here quickly!"

Zoe stopped watching the seagulls dive and swoop. She ran over to Carlos. He was looking at a long, brown-gray, fishy kind of animal.

"What is it?" asked Zoe.

"I think it's a small shark," said Carlos.

Zoe looked at the sharp teeth and pointy fins. She said, "I think you're right."

"Is it still alive?" asked Carlos.

"I think so," answered Zoe. "We'll have to get it in the water soon, though."

"Let's go home," said Carlos. "Mom and Dad can help us to safely put the shark back into the ocean."

_____

_____

_____

_____

_____

Designer Shoes

Directions: Use the information you see in the picture below to fill in the graph with the correct information. The "dots" column has already been filled in for you. Look at the graph, and write the answers to the questions on the lines below.

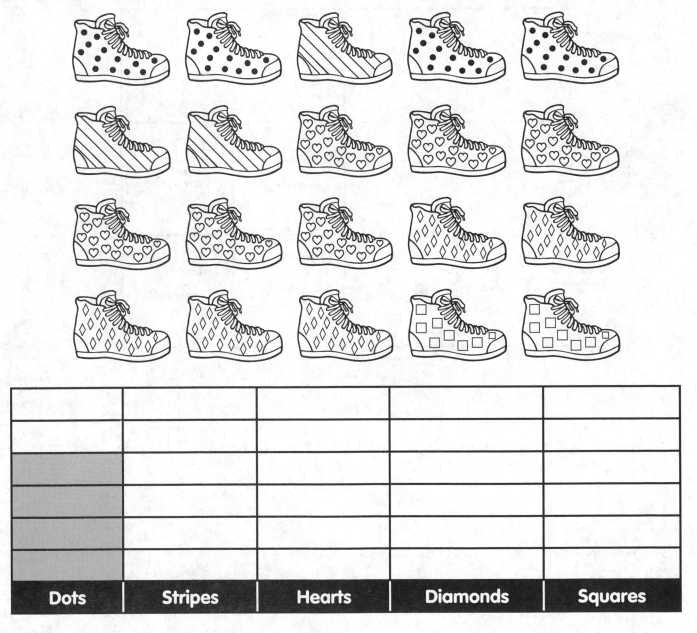

Dots	**Stripes**	**Hearts**	**Diamonds**	**Squares**

1. Which shoes did you find most often? _____

2. Which shoes did you find least often? _____

3. How many shoes did you find altogether? _____

Which number Am I?

Directions: Read each clue. Put an **X** on the number(s) that do not fit each clue. After reading all of the clues, there will be one number left.

805,457	879	80,121	579
2,157	39,643	29,253	144,384
66,175	9,780	7,418	102

Clues

1. When my digits are added together, the total number is a number greater than 20 but less than 30.

2. There is one 7 in my number.

3. There are more than 3 digits in my number.

4. If you add and subtract each number in order, the answer is less than 10. (Example: 579 is 5 + 7 – 9 = 3)

5. The number is higher than 10,000.

6. Which number am I?_____

It's Easy to Divide!

Learning how to divide is easier if you think of division as repeated subtraction. For example, you can solve the following division word problem using repeated subtraction.

Jim has invented a new game using jacks. A total of 18 jacks are used to play the game. In order to play, each player must start with 3 jacks. How many people can play the game?

Think: How many 3s can I subtract from 18?

$$18 - 3 - 3 - 3 - 3 - 3 - 3 = 0$$

| player 1 | player 2 | player 3 | player 4 | player 5 | player 6 |

6 groups of 3

$$3\overline{)18}$$ with quotient 6

Directions: Use the multiplication chart on page 104 to help you find the answers to these problems. Use repeated subtraction to check your answers.

1. How many 8s can you subtract from 32? _____

2. How many 5s can you subtract from 40? _____

3. How many 6s can you subtract from 24? _____

4. How many 7s can you subtract from 42? _____

5. How many 8s can you subtract from 56? _____

Seeing and Hearing

A **consonant digraph** is two consonants that make one sound, like /sh/ in *shop*, /ch/ in *chip*, /th/ in *that*, /wh/ in *who*, and /ck/ in *pick*.

Directions: Say the name of each picture. Circle the consonant digraph that you hear.

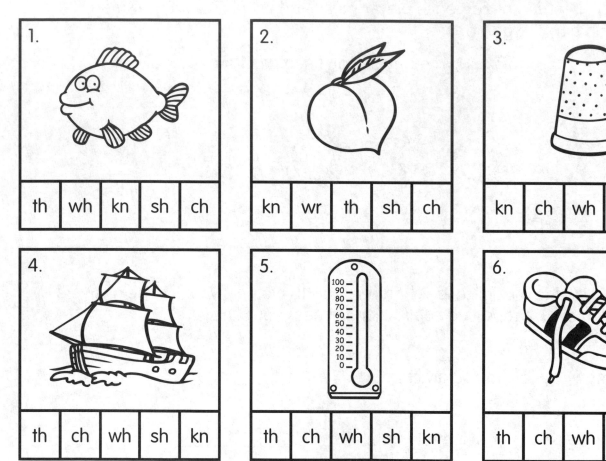

1.

| th | wh | kn | sh | ch |

2.

| kn | wr | th | sh | ch |

3.

| kn | ch | wh | sh | th |

4.

| th | ch | wh | sh | kn |

5.

| th | ch | wh | sh | kn |

6.

| th | ch | wh | sh | kn |

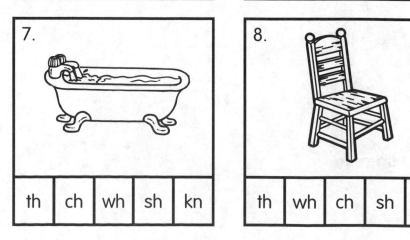

7.

| th | ch | wh | sh | kn |

8.

| th | wh | ch | sh | kn |

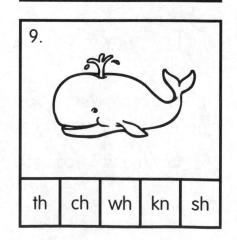

9.

| th | ch | wh | kn | sh |

Grouping

Directions: Use different colors or patterns to make equal groups. Complete the word and number sentence to record results.

1. 5 in each group

There are _____ groups of 5 hearts.

$25 \div 5 =$ _____

2. 4 in each group

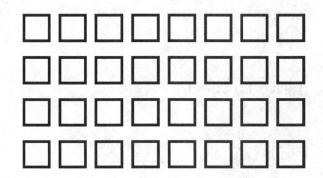

There are _____ groups of 4 squares.

$32 \div 4 =$ _____

3. 3 in each group

There are _____ groups of 3 stars.

$30 \div 3 =$ _____

4. 2 in each group

There are _____ groups of 2 triangles.

$18 \div 2 =$ _____

Lists

Punctuation Rule

Use commas to separate words in a series.

Directions: Use the Word Bank at the bottom of the page to complete each sentence. Be sure to separate the words in each series with commas. The first one has been done for you.

1. Would you like _____pizza_____ , _____pasta_____ , or _____steak_____ for dinner?

2. I like to play _____ _____ and _____.

3. I have _____ _____ and _____ crayons.

4. I saw _____ _____ and _____ at the zoo.

5. Is this shape a _____ _____ or _____?

6. I practice on _____ _____ and _____.

Word Bank

~~pizza pasta steak~~	lions tigers bears
Monday Friday Sunday	red blue green
triangle square circle	soccer golf tennis

Find the Number

Math

Directions: Color the correct number of items.

1. Color $\frac{3}{4}$ of the 16 shoes. $\frac{3}{4}$ of 16 = _____ shoes.

2. Color $\frac{2}{5}$ of the 15 cookies. $\frac{2}{5}$ of 15 = _____ cookies.

3. Color $\frac{1}{2}$ of the 20 skateboards. $\frac{1}{2}$ of 20 = _____ skateboards.

Movie Poster

What if you were allowed to turn your favorite book into a movie? What famous director would direct it? Who would produce it? Which actors would portray which characters? How would the graphics on your poster entice people to come see the movie?

In the space below, design a poster for the film version of your favorite book. Make sure to choose an exciting picture that ties in with a character or theme from the book. Cast the movie, and list the actors' names on your poster. Don't forget the director and producer. What rating would this movie have? Include it on your poster.

Share Evenly

Directions: Complete the problems.

1. You have 15 candies left in a bag. You want to divide the candy among your three friends. Draw circles showing the candies divided evenly among your friends. How many candies does each friend have? _____

2. Bryson bought 20 marbles. He wants to share the marbles with his friend Jessie. Draw circles showing the marbles divided evenly between Bryson and Jessie. How many marbles does each have? _____

3. Patty had 12 flowers to give to her 4 friends. Draw circles showing how Patty handed out the flowers evenly among her friends. How many flowers does each friend have? _____

Sizzling Sounds

Onomatopoeia is the use of words that sound like what they are describing, such as *buzz, swish,* and *growl*.

Directions: Create onomatopoeia poems. Choose a sound word from the Word Bank, and write it next to the object it describes.

Word Bank

baas	meows	pitter-patter	swoosh
cracks	neighs	quacks	woofs

Animals

A cat _____ .

A duck _____ .

A dog _____ .

A sheep _____ .

A horse _____ .

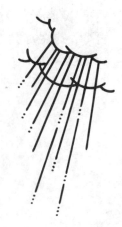

The Weather

The wind went _____ .

The thunder _____ .

The rain goes _____ .

Brain Busters

Directions: Write the equation(s) using the correct math symbol (+, −, x, ÷) to solve each problem.

1. Number of legs on three dogs	2. Number of eyes on one person	3. A dozen eggs placed equally in three bowls
4. Number of fingers on three hands	5. How many eyes are on five three-eyed aliens?	6. Number of nickels it takes to make one quarter
7. Number of cookies in $\frac{1}{2}$ a dozen	8. There are ten points. Each star has five points. How many stars?	9. How many dimes are in one dollar?

Spell a Word

Directions: Use letters from each set to spell a word. You will not use all the letters. The first one has been done for you.

1. A B C D E F H	FACE
2. I J K L M N O P	
3. O R S T U Y M A	
4. A C E G D K M O	
5. B D F H N A O E	
6. E U T R L D S Y	
7. A F G M P R E O	
8. I B D K E H L U	
9. G I C O M L N A	
10. K I A B G S L C	
11. E L A G T O N F	
12. S E G C M H B O	
13. T A O E M L N R	
14. R I T S L N M E	
15. Y E B D G F O U	

Writing Fractions

A **fraction** is a part (or parts) of a whole item or shape.

 $\dfrac{2}{3}$

 $\dfrac{1}{5}$

Two parts out of three are shaded.

One part out of five is shaded.

Directions: Look at each shape. Write the fraction that tells how many parts of the whole object are shaded. The first one has been done for you.

1.

$\dfrac{1}{3}$

2.

3.
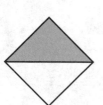

4.
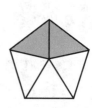

5.

6.

7.

8.

Making Sentences

A **sentence** must make sense and must contain a subject and a verb.

Directions: Circle the endings that would make sentences.

1. The teacher
   some white chalk.
   told us to stand.
   read us a story.
   a television.

2. A large dog
   barked at the cat.
   with four legs.
   chewed the bone.
   very savage.

3. The small bird
   built a nest in the tree.
   on the lawn.
   is singing a song.
   black feathers.

Directions: Add words of your own to make sentences. The first one has been done for you.

4. dog   chewed   bone

   A hungry dog eagerly chewed a juicy bone.

5. boy   lost   dollar

   _____

6. truck   crashed   fence

   _____

Fraction Practice

Math

Directions: Write the following fractions in standard form.

Example: 3 out of 4 ___$\frac{3}{4}$___

1. 6 out of 10 _____

2. 2 tenths _____

3. 5 eighths _____

4. seven-eighths _____

5. ten-twelfths _____

6. 10 out of 100 _____

7. one-half _____

8. 20 out of 100 _____

Directions: Order these fractions from smallest to largest. Remember, the larger the denominator (number under the line), the smaller the part.

9. $\frac{1}{3}$, $\frac{1}{10}$, $\frac{1}{4}$ _____

10. $\frac{3}{10}$, $\frac{5}{10}$, $\frac{8}{10}$ _____

11. $\frac{2}{4}$, $\frac{2}{5}$, $\frac{2}{3}$ _____

12. $\frac{1}{8}$, $\frac{7}{8}$, $\frac{3}{8}$ _____

13. 2, $1\frac{1}{2}$, $4\frac{1}{2}$ _____

14. $\frac{1}{5}$, $\frac{1}{6}$, $\frac{1}{2}$ _____

Synonyms

Synonyms are words that are the same or almost the same in meaning. For example, *pretty* is a synonym for *beautiful*.

Directions: Complete the sentences using words from the Word Bank. Write a word that makes sense in the top sentence. Then, complete the next sentence with a synonym. Write that word on the second line.

Word Bank

attractive	friends	infant	shop
baby	gift	present	silently
buddies	handsome	quietly	store

1. The two girls are_____ .

   The two girls are_____ .

2. The _____ is starting to crawl.

   The _____ is starting to crawl.

3. The class worked _____ .

   The class worked _____ .

4. We will buy his present at a toy _____ .

   We will buy his present at a toy _____ .

5. I am going to wrap my _____ .

   I am going to wrap my _____ .

6. Her boyfriend is very _____ .

   Her boyfriend is very _____ .

Name That Fraction

Directions: Name the fraction that is shaded.

1.
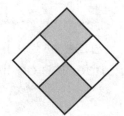
_____

2.
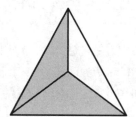
_____

3.
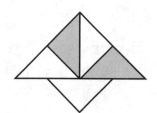
_____

4.

_____

5.
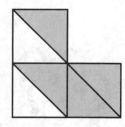
_____

6.
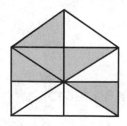
_____

7.
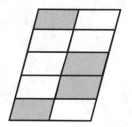
_____

8.
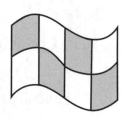
_____

9.
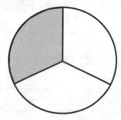
_____

10.

_____

11.
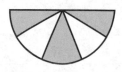
_____

12.
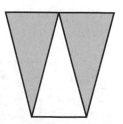
_____

Show Me

What if a strange space vehicle landed in your friend's backyard, and instead of letting you come see it, your friend said to you, "I'll just tell you about it, and then you won't have to see it." How would you feel? Wouldn't you rather go see it yourself? Good writing lets the reader "see" it for him or herself. Good writing doesn't tell; it shows. When it shows, the reader forms a picture in his or her own mind.

Directions: Circle the sentences below that let you "see" what is described. Underline the sentences that just tell you about it. Rewrite the sentences you underline on the lines below. The first one has been done for you.

1. There was a tall, blue vase full of bright purple daisies on the table.

2. Alicia heard a bird.

3. Maria saw a tiny, white dog with muddy paws and a nervous tail.

4. Ms. Connolly is nice.

5. I saw Mr. Olsen buy lunch for Matt after he forgot his.

6. I live in a house.

7. That's a noisy car.

_____

_____

_____

_____

A Fair Share

A **fraction** is a part of something. Most things can be divided into smaller or equal parts.

 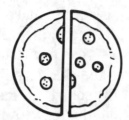 

Directions: Follow the instructions below.

1. Draw a circle around the picture that shows the fraction $\frac{1}{2}$.

2. Place an **X** on the picture that shows the fraction $\frac{1}{4}$.

3. Divide the circle into two equal parts.

4. Divide the square into four equal parts.

5. Divide the rectangle into three equal parts.

 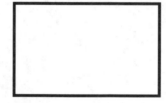 

# Farmer Grey's Morning

Directions: Read the story. Then, complete the web below by writing a title for the story in the center circle and the main events in the surrounding circles.

Farmer Grey woke up as the sun was rising. He had a lot of work to do. He went outside and looked at the sky. A storm was brewing in the distance. He knew he needed to hurry. So he went to the barn and gave fresh hay to the horses. He cleaned the pigpen and fed the chickens. He checked the hen house and collected the eggs from the nests. He ran inside and put the eggs in the refrigerator. Then, he hiked out to the pasture to check on the cows. As Farmer Grey headed back to the house, the sky grew dark, and it started to rain. He made it to the house as the storm showered down on him. He opened the door and smelled eggs and bacon cooking in the kitchen. All that work and the day had only just begun!

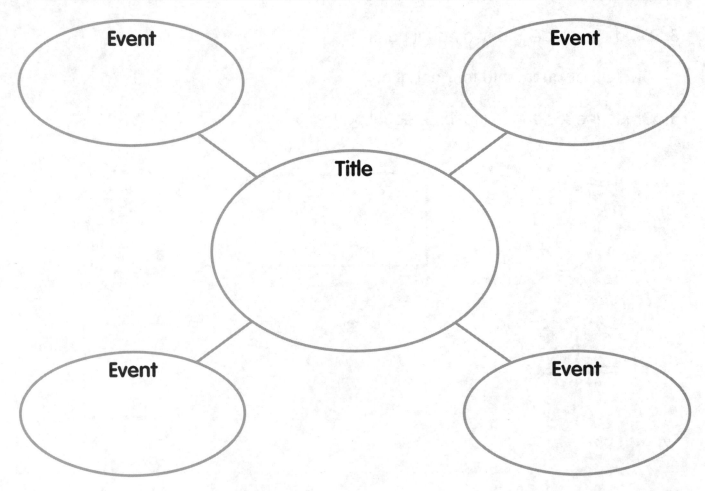

Event

Event

Title

Event

Event

What's the Fraction?

Directions: Identify the fraction. Then, color the puzzle.

halves = red   **thirds** = blue   **fourths** = yellow   **fifths** = green

Which Comes First?

Directions: Look at the pictures below. Write their names on the lines underneath them. Then, put the picture names in ABC order at the bottom of the page.

_____ _____ _____ _____ _____

_____ _____ _____ _____ _____

1. _____

2. _____

3. _____

4. _____

5. _____

6. _____

7. _____

8. _____

9. _____

10. _____

70

Word Problems

Steps to Solving Word Problems

1. **Read** the word problem a few times.
2. **Underline** the words that give you facts or clues about whether to add, subtract, multiply, or divide.
3. **Draw** a picture to show the solution, or use real items to solve the problem.
4. **Write** the math sentence, and solve the problem.

Directions: Draw a picture, and write out the math sentence to solve each word problem below. The first one has been started for you.

1. Robert has three marbles in each bag. He has two bags. How many marbles does Robert have in all?

    $2 \times 3 =$

    or

    $3 + 3 =$

2. Jackie had 19 footballs. His friends took 8 of the footballs. How many does Jackie have left?

3. The Tigers scored the following points: 9, 7, 5, 3, and 7. What was the sum of their points?

4. Susie has 21 tennis balls. She would like to give them to her friends so each one has the same number of tennis balls. She has 7 friends. How many can she give to each friend?

Antonyms

Antonyms are words that are opposite or almost opposite in meaning.
For example, *up* is an antonym of *down*.

Directions: Find a word in the box that means the opposite of each picture below.
Print the word on the line.

awake   day   down   dry   go   solid

1.

2.

3.

4.

5.

6.

Number Sentences

Directions: Read each word problem. Write the number sentence. Then, find the answer.

1. At the circus, Kenny saw 16 tigers and 27 monkeys. How many animals did he see in all?

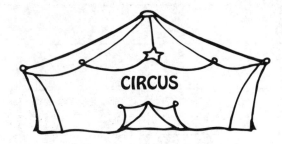

_____ + _____ = _____

2. When Lyla went to the tidepools, she counted 28 starfish and 46 shells. How many things did she see in all?

_____ + _____ = _____

3. Jason bought a pair of shoes for $53.00. Clark bought a pair for $28.00. What is the difference paid?

_____ − _____ = _____

4. Jill counted 83 ants near an anthill. Jack counted 65. What is the difference in the ants counted?

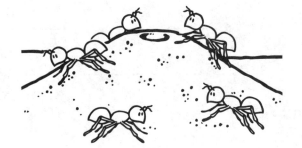

_____ − _____ = _____

Amazing Adverbs

> **Adverbs** are words that tell about, or describe, verbs.
>
> **Examples:** The horse ran *quickly*.
>
> I walked *quietly*.
>
> The author wrote *well*.

Directions: Write the adverb that describes the underlined verb in each sentence.

1. Anne and Tom <u>work</u> hard. _____

2. Elise and Erica <u>ate</u> quickly. _____

3. Ethan <u>listens</u> intently. _____

4. The horse <u>ran</u> fast. _____

5. Cows <u>eat</u> grass slowly. _____

6. Mrs. Smith <u>yelled</u> loudly. _____

Directions: Write an adverb in each blank to describe the verb.

7. jumped _____

8. flew _____

9. skipped _____

10. slept _____

Your Own Words

Math

Directions: Read the following word problems. In your own words, write down what you need to find out. Then, use the "Steps to Solving Word Problems" on page 71 to help you solve each problem.

1. Your best friend has a bag with 203 marbles. You have 164 marbles in your backpack. How many marbles do you and your friend have altogether?

   I have to find out_____

   _____ .   Solution: _____

2. You have a bag with 25 candies in it. Sarah has a jumbo bag with 5 times as many candies in it. How many candies does Sarah have?

   I have to find out_____

   _____ .   Solution: _____

3. Your little sister has 30 dimes in her piggy bank. How many dollar bills could she get for those 30 dimes?

   I have to find out_____

   _____ .   Solution: _____

4. A baseball mitt costs $18.89. You have saved $9.40. How much more money do you need to buy the mitt?

   I have to find out_____

   _____ .   Solution: _____

Giant Bubbles

Directions: Read the information below. Then, answer the questions that follow.

Here is a great recipe for a hot day. You should have everything you need around your house.

You will need:

☼ dishpan or cookie sheet ☼ 2 tbsp. dish soap

☼ water ☼ wire hangers

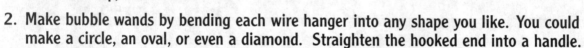

1. Fill the dishpan or cookie sheet with warm water and dish soap, and mix well.

2. Make bubble wands by bending each wire hanger into any shape you like. You could make a circle, an oval, or even a diamond. Straighten the hooked end into a handle.

3. Dip your wand into the bubble mixture, and wave it around in the air. You should have giant bubbles!

1. According to the story, making giant bubbles is a good thing to do
   a. during the summer. c. during recess.
   b. at a dress-up party. d. during the winter.

2. What is the second step in the instructions?
   a. Make a bubble wand out of a hanger.
   b. Wash the dishpan or cookie sheet.
   c. Dip the wand into the bubble mixture.
   d. Fill a dishpan or cookie sheet with warm water.

3. How many different things will you need to make giant bubbles?
   a. seven c. four
   b. six d. three

4. The best way to answer the question right before this one is to
   a. guess the number of things you will need.
   b. imagine that you are making the bubbles.
   c. count the number of things on the "you will need" list.
   d. count the number of steps in the instructions.

76

Key Words

Directions: Underline the key word(s) in each problem. Solve the problem, and write the answer in the box. The first one has been done for you.

1. Rosie took <u>12 pictures</u> of her cat and <u>15 pictures</u> of her dog. How many pictures <u>altogether</u> did Rosie take of her animals?

$$\begin{array}{r} 12 \\ +\ 15 \\ \hline 27 \end{array}$$

27 pictures

2. There were 8 monkeys in the tree and 4 monkeys on the log. How many more monkeys were in the tree than on the log?

3. Mom bought 30 large plastic cups and 15 small plastic cups for the party. How many total cups did Mom buy?

4. The library had a summer reading contest. The girls read 139 books, and the boys read 128 books. What is the sum of the books the boys and girls read this summer?

5. Mrs. Simmons bought 50 pencils at the store. She gave 26 of the pencils to her students. How many pencils does Mrs. Simmons have left?

6. The gardener planted 44 flowers in the first row and 40 flowers in the second row. What is the difference between the number of flowers in the two rows?

Super Synonyms

Directions: Write a synonym above each underlined word. Use a thesaurus if needed. Then, copy the story on the lines below.

One day, a <u>man</u> and his <u>child</u> left their <u>house</u>. They <u>walked</u>

to the park. They wanted to play. They <u>ran</u> through

the grass and <u>laughed</u>. The <u>man</u> and the <u>child</u> <u>saw</u>

birds in the trees. They <u>saw</u> a <u>pretty</u> butterfly float by.

It was a <u>great</u> day. On the way home, the child saw his <u>friend</u>.

He <u>said</u>, "Hi, David!" They both <u>smiled</u>.

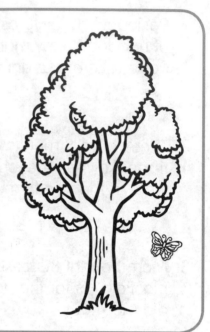

_____

_____

_____

_____

_____

_____

_____

Fireworks Sudoku

Directions: Fill every square with an indicated color. No color can be repeated in a column, row, or box.

R = Red	**Y** = Yellow	**B** = Blue
O = Orange	**G** = Green	**P** = Purple

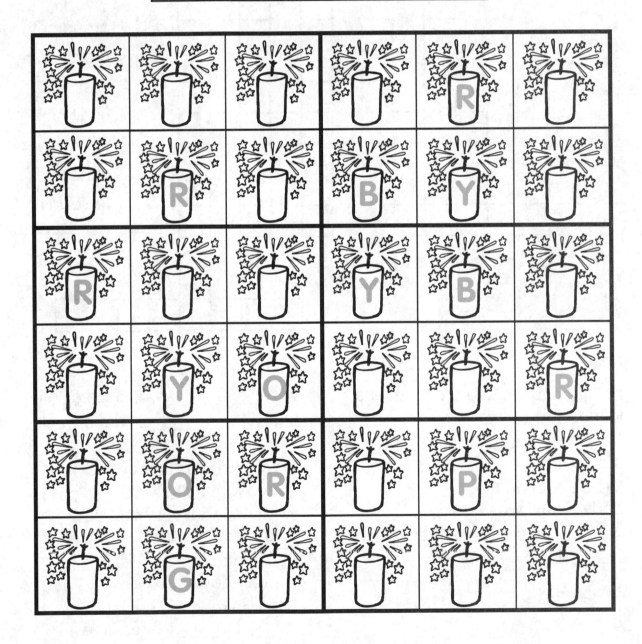

Compound Crossword

Directions: Complete each clue below with a compound word. Use the Word Bank to help you.

Word Bank

butterfly
cupboard
doorbell
grandmother
grasshoppers
lipstick
mailbox
newspaper
raincoat
tablecloth

Across

1. My mom told me to drop the letters in the _____.
8. Before Sandra put out the plates, she put on the _____.
9. Steven opened the _____ and found it was empty.
10. Annette put on her mother's _____.

Down

2. A _____ was once a caterpillar.
3. My _____ spent a week at our house.
4. My dad likes to read the _____ every morning.
5. Maria liked watching the _____ jump on her lawn.
6. Bob had to wear his _____ every day this week.
7. Karen rang the neighbor's _____ three times.

Rounding Numbers

Directions: Solve each word problem by rounding each number to the nearest ten and then adding or subtracting. Show your work in the space provided. The first one has been done for you.

1. Jason invited 39 girls and 22 boys to his party. How many children did Jason invite in all?

    The number 39 is rounded to 40. The number 22 is rounded to 20.

    ___60___ children were invited to the party.

    $$\begin{array}{r} 40 \\ + 20 \\ \hline 60 \end{array}$$

2. Mariah bought 152 balloons, 127 party hats, and 213 candles for the party. How many party items did Mariah buy in all?

    Mariah bought_____ party items in all.

3. Beau sent out 185 invitations. Eighty-seven people said "yes." The rest said "no." How many people said "no?"

    _____ people said "no."

4. Lucy set out 210 green jellybeans, 315 red jellybeans, and 57 orange jellybeans. How many jellybeans did Lucy set out in all?

    Lucy set out_____ jellybeans.

5. Sprinkles were put on 3 cupcakes. The children used 567 sprinkles in all. The first cupcake had 237 sprinkles. The second cupcake had 197. How many sprinkles did the third cupcake have?

    The third cupcake had _____ sprinkles.

6. Darts were played at the party. Ben scored 222 points. Jacob scored 303 points. Elena scored 368 points. How many points were scored in all?

    _____ points were scored in all.

Adding Adjectives

Directions: Add adjectives, or describing words, in the spaces below. Then, draw pictures to match your descriptions.

a _____ _____ apple

a _____ _____ house

a _____ _____ pencil

a _____ _____ tree

a _____ _____ monster

a _____ _____ vacation

Snack Bar Math

Directions: Read the Snack Bar Menu. Then, solve the word problems. First, estimate how much each order will cost. Then, compute the total cost.

Snack Bar Menu

SANDWICHES		DRINKS		SNACKS	
hamburger	$1.12	soda	$0.75	chips	$0.60
cheeseburger	$1.46	juice	$0.64	apple	$0.38
fish	$1.24	water	$0.52	pretzels	$0.22
chicken	$1.39	milk	$0.48	popcorn	$0.56
peanut butter	$0.98			Jelly Gillies	$0.43

1. DeMarco was very hungry. He ordered one cheeseburger, one bag of chips, one apple, and a bottle of water. What was his total cost?

   Estimate: _____   Answer: _____

2. Dion only wanted snacks and a drink. He ordered one bag of pretzels, one bag of popcorn, and a can of soda. What was his total cost?

   Estimate: _____   Answer: _____

3. David decided he was hungry, too, so he ordered one fish sandwich, two packages of Jelly Gillies, and one bottle of water. What was his total cost?

   Estimate: _____   Answer: _____

4. Boyd and Terrell were hungry after working at the Snack Bar. They bought one hamburger, one chicken sandwich, two cans of soda, one container of milk, two bags of popcorn, and one box of Jelly Gillies. What was their total cost?

   Estimate: _____   Answer: _____

5. Susan walked to the Snack Bar and ordered some food. She bought one peanut butter sandwich, one juice, two bags of pretzels, and one apple. What was her total cost?

   Estimate: _____   Answer: _____

Rodeo Sounds

In a **diphthong**, two vowels blend together to make one sound. The diphthongs *oi* and *oy* stand for the vowel sound in *toil* and *toy*. The diphthongs *ow* and *ou* stand for the vowel sound in *cow* and *mouse*. The diphthong *ew* stands for the vowel sound in *new*.

Directions: Use the words in the Word Bank to complete the story.

Word Bank

boy	cowboys	grew	newspaper	Roy
choice	crowd	loud	noise	town

Can you hear the _____ ? That _____ sound is
⠀⠀⠀⠀⠀⠀⠀⠀⠀⠀⠀⠀⠀⠀⠀⠀⠀⠀⠀1⠀⠀⠀⠀⠀⠀⠀⠀⠀⠀⠀⠀⠀⠀⠀⠀⠀⠀⠀⠀⠀2

coming from the fairground. A _____ is gathering because the
⠀⠀⠀⠀⠀⠀⠀⠀⠀⠀⠀⠀⠀⠀⠀⠀⠀⠀⠀⠀⠀⠀⠀⠀⠀⠀3

rodeo is in _____ !
⠀⠀⠀⠀⠀⠀⠀⠀⠀⠀⠀4

I read about one of the _____ in the _____ .
⠀⠀⠀⠀⠀⠀⠀⠀⠀⠀⠀⠀⠀⠀⠀⠀⠀⠀⠀5⠀⠀⠀⠀⠀⠀⠀⠀⠀⠀⠀⠀⠀⠀⠀⠀⠀⠀6

His name is _____ .
⠀⠀⠀⠀⠀⠀⠀⠀⠀⠀7

He learned to ride a horse when

he was a _____ .
⠀⠀⠀⠀⠀⠀⠀⠀8

After he _____ up,
⠀⠀⠀⠀⠀⠀⠀⠀9

it was his _____ to be a cowboy.
⠀⠀⠀⠀⠀⠀⠀⠀10

Solving Problems

Directions: Solve each problem. Show your work.

1. I had a whole pie.
   I cut it in half.
   How many pieces
   of pie do I have now?

   I have _____ piece(s) of pie.

2. Rocky ordered a pizza.
   The pizza was cut
   into four equal pieces.
   Rocky ate half of the pizza.
   How many pieces did Rocky eat?

   Rocky ate _____ piece(s) of pizza.

3. Ricky had nine marbles.
   He kept $\frac{1}{3}$. He gave
   $\frac{1}{3}$ to Sonya and $\frac{1}{3}$
   to Len. How many marbles does
   each person have now?

   Each person has _____ marble(s).

4. Marilyn had five houses.
   She sold $\frac{1}{5}$ of them.
   How many houses did
   she keep?

   Marilyn kept _____ house(s).

In Charge

Directions: Create a poem by completing the page below. Remember, a poem doesn't have to rhyme!

If I were in charge of the world,

I'd cancel _____,

_____,

_____, and also

_____.

If I were in charge of the world,

There'd be _____

_____,

_____,

_____, and

_____.

If I were in charge of the world,

You wouldn't have _____.

You wouldn't have _____.

You wouldn't have _____ or

_____.

You wouldn't even have _____.

If I were in charge of the world,

_____

_____.

And a person who sometimes forgot _____

And sometimes forgot _____

Would still be allowed to be in charge of the world.

86

Money Madness!

Directions: Solve each money riddle.

1. Michelle has five coins in her pocket. Together the coins equal 47¢. What coins does Michelle have in her pocket?

2. Kevin has three coins in his pocket. The coins are all of the same value. The coins equal 75¢. What coins does Kevin have in his pocket?

3. Matt has four coins in his pocket. The coins are all of different values. The coins equal 41¢. What coins does Matt have in his pocket?

4. Corinne has two coins in her pocket. The coins are of the same value and equal $1.00. What coins does Corinne have in her pocket?

5. Riley has six coins of three different values. Together, the coins equal 80¢. What coins does Riley have in her pocket?

6. Brandon has seven coins in his pocket. Together, the coins equal 51¢. What coins does Brandon have in his pocket?

Using Schedules

Schedules play an important part in our lives. We have schedules for each day at school. We have schedules for sports days and swim meets. From a schedule, you can work out how long things take.

Directions: This schedule shows what Luke's class does on a Friday. Read it, and then answer the questions below.

Schedule — Friday	
Time	**Subject**
9:00 a.m.	Weekly assembly—Room 3C
9:30 a.m.	Story writing
10:15 a.m.	Math
10:45 a.m.	Free reading
11:00 a.m.	**RECESS**
11:20 a.m.	Art
12:20 p.m.	Computers with Ms. Grey
12:45 p.m.	**LUNCH**
1:30 p.m.	Quiet reading time
2:00 p.m.	Science
2:30 p.m.	P.E. with Mr. Castle
3:10 p.m.	End of classes

1. What time does Luke start school? _____

2. How long is recess? _____ minutes

3. Which lesson is the longest? _____

4. Who teaches P.E. to Luke's class? _____

5. When does math finish? _____

6. What does the class have at 1:30 p.m.? The class has _____.

Sun Sudoku

Directions: Fill every square with an indicated color. No color can be repeated in a column, row, or box.

R = Red	**Y** = Yellow	**B** = Blue
O = Orange	**G** = Green	**P** = Purple

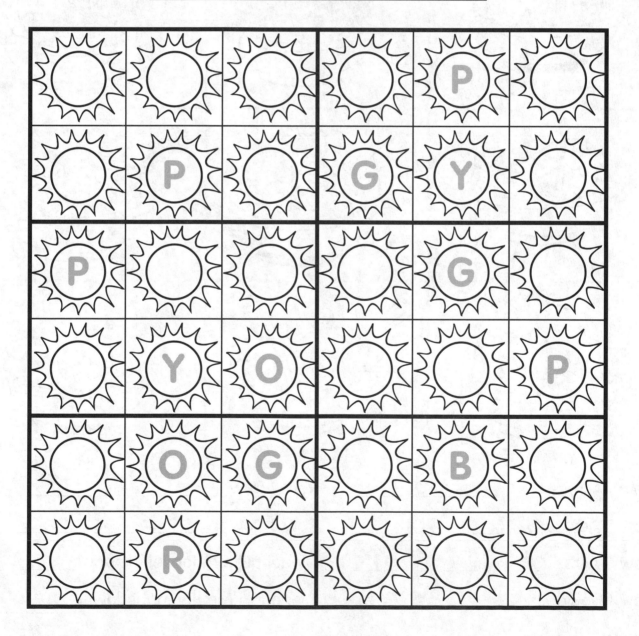

Ice-Cream Sundaes

Directions: Each picture has something in common with the other pictures in its row. In the top row across, each vanilla sundae has chocolate syrup. Look at the other rows across, down, and diagonally. Find the thing that makes each row the same. Fill in your answers at the bottom of the page.

Row 1 Across: _____

Row 2 Across: _____

Row 3 Across: _____

Row 1 Down: _____

Row 2 Down: _____

Row 3 Down: _____

Diagonal (from top left down): _____

Diagonal (from top right down): _____

All About Me

Something I Like About Myself:

_____

_____

_____

_____

My Favorite Song:

_____

_____

_____

_____

My Best Family Vacation:

_____

_____

_____

Summer Reading List

○ **Ghost of the Southern Belle: A Sea Tale** by Odds Bodkin

Captain LeNoir's ship may have crashed on rocks and sank, but he and his ghostly crew continue to haunt the waters where they met their demise.

○ **The Treekeepers** by Susan Britton

This is a fantasy story about a young street urchin named Bird who sets out to find her real father but meets trouble and makes friends along the way.

○ **Keeper of the Doves** by Betsy Byars

Four sisters tease and torment an old man who once saved their father's life as they learn about loyalty and life.

○ **The Janitor's Boy** by Andrew Clements

Fifth-grader Jack finds himself the object of ridicule and practical jokes when his father's job becomes known around school.

○ **Granny Torelli Makes Soup** by Sharon Creech

Granny Torelli imparts life lessons and advice to her granddaughter while making and sharing Italian food.

○ **A Door in the Woods** by James Dashner

Book one in the Jimmy Fincher saga shows Jimmy witnessing something while perched in a tree in the woods that turns his world upside down. The following month is full of adventure and legends come to life!

○ **The Lemonade War** by Jacqueline Davies

Evan's little sister is skipping third grade. Not only is she skipping third grade, but she's also going to be in Evan's fourth-grade classroom at the beginning of the year! This starts a war to see which of them can make the most money in the week before school starts.

○ **The Miraculous Journey of Edward Tulane** by Kate DeCamillo

This is an enchanting and enriching story about the journey of Edward Tulane, a toy rabbit made entirely of fine china, as he goes from living a life of luxury to finding true friendships and love in circumstances he never imagined.

○ **The Gollywhopper Games** by Jody Feldman

The Golly Toy & Game Company's Ultimate Championship is the only thing standing between Gil Goodson and true happiness. Can he beat the other kids on live TV?

Making the Most of Summertime Reading

When reading these books with your child, you may wish to ask the questions below. The sharing of questions and answers will enhance and improve your child's reading comprehension skills.

○ Why did you choose this book to read?

○ Name a character from the story that you like. Why do you like him or her?

○ Where does the story take place? Do you want to vacation there?

○ Name a problem that occurs in the story. How is it resolved?

○ What is the best part of the story so far? Describe it!

○ What do you think is going to happen next in the story? Make a prediction!

○ Who are the important characters in the story? Why are they important?

○ What is the book about?

○ What are two things you have learned by reading this book?

○ Would you tell your friend to read this book? Why or why not?

Summer Reading List

✿ **The Green Dog: A Mostly True Story** by Suzanne Fisher Staples

A young girl has an imaginary dog-friend, "Jeff," because she's always wanted a dog. When a black-and-white stray comes into her life, she knows he's the dog for her. After a while, trouble arises when her dog has a way of getting into mischief, and the family has to make a tough decision.

✿ **Sir Reginald's Logbook** by Matt Hammill

Sir Reginald writes about his search for the mysterious "Lost Tablet of Illusion." Is it in the deepest jungle? Is it on the tallest peak? Or is it some place more familiar?

✿ **How Strong Is It?** by Ben Hillman

This is a nonfiction book that compares the strength of twenty-two different objects or animals, including glue, gravity, and spider webs.

✿ **Babymouse #9: Monster Mash** by Jennifer L. Holm and Matthew Holm

This graphic novel will surely capture your attention! Babymouse wants to have the best Halloween party and the best Halloween costume. But she runs into some obstacles along the way.

✿ **Dragon Keepers #1: Dragon in the Sock Drawer** by Kate Klimo

Jesse finds a "thunder egg" while out hunting for rocks one afternoon. Soon, something is asking to be let out of the egg…and the adventure begins!

✿ **Savvy** by Ingrid Law

Mib, who is almost a teenager, is in a magical family when disaster strikes her Poppa. She only hopes her magical power, which hasn't blossomed yet, can save him!

✿ **Pictures of Hollis Woods** by Patricia Reilly Giff

Hollis, an orphan, has always wished for a family and one day is adopted by a retired art teacher for whom she becomes a caregiver.

✿ **Sideways Stories from Wayside School** by Louis Sachar

Wayside School was built wrong; it should have thirty classrooms side by side, but they were built on top of each other instead! This collection of short stories introduces you to the students and staff of Wayside School—characters you'll never forget!

✿ **Where I Live** by Eileen Spinelli

This is a touching tale about a family forced to move from their beloved home when the father loses his job. Will they ever feel comfortable in their new home?

✿ **Piper Reed, Navy Brat** by Kimberly Willis Holt

Piper Reed's father is in the Navy and has already moved her family around more times than she can count. Will she and her sisters survive the latest move to Pensacola, Florida?

Fun Ways to Love Books

Here are some fun ways that your child can expand on his or her reading. Most of these ideas will involve both you and your child; however, the wording has been directed towards your child because we want him or her to be inspired to love books.

Design a Bookmark

You can design a bookmark for your favorite book, and then use it in other books to remind you of a great reading experience. Use a strip of colorful paper and include the title, the author, and a picture of something that happened in the book.

Write to the Author

Many authors love to hear from their readers, especially when they hear what people liked best about their books. You can write to an author and send your letter in care of the book's publisher. The publisher's address is listed directly after the title page. Or you may go to the author's Web site and follow the directions for how to send the author a letter. (To make sure your author is still living, do a search on the Internet, typing the author's name into a search engine.)

A Comic Book

Turn your favorite book into a comic book. Fold at least two sheets of paper in half, and staple them so they make a book. With a ruler and pencil, draw boxes across each page to look like blank comic strips. Then, draw the story of your book as if it were a comic. Draw pictures of your characters, and have words coming out of their mouths—just as in a real comic strip.

Always Take a Book

Maybe you've had to wait with your parents in line at the post office or in the vet's waiting room with nothing to do. If you get into the habit of bringing a book with you wherever you go, you'll always have something exciting to do! Train yourself to always take a good book. You might want to carry a small backpack or shoulder bag—something that allows you to carry a book easily from place to place. Don't forget a bookmark!

Learn a New Skill

What skills are mentioned in your favorite book? Perhaps a character learns to ride a unicycle. Other characters may create beautiful pottery, learn to juggle, take black-and-white photographs, train dogs, or bake five-layer cakes. Identify a skill mentioned in your book. Gather together the materials you'll need to learn this skill. Keep in mind that learning a new skill may take several weeks or months. Commit to practicing this skill at least twice a week. Keep a journal detailing your growing abilities. Finally, organize a talent show to demonstrate your newfound skill!

Bookmark Your Words

Make summertime reading lots of fun with these reading log glasses. Have your child fill in the glasses after his or her daily reading. For younger children, you may need to help them fill in the information. Or, as an alternative, they can draw a picture of something they read from that day. Once they have completed the glasses, they can cut them out and use them as bookmarks.

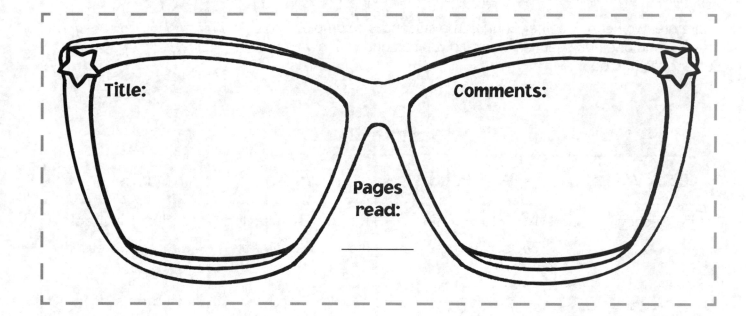

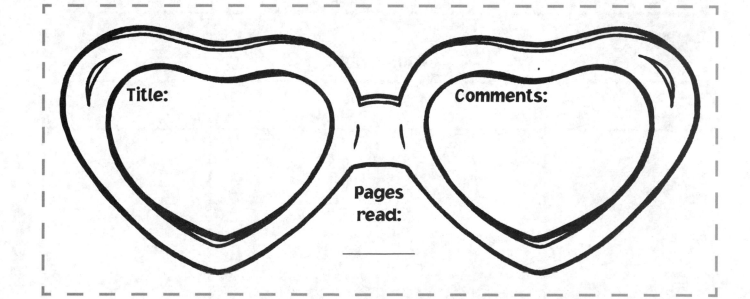

This page may be reproduced as many times as needed.

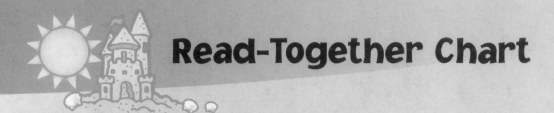

Read-Together Chart

Does your father read books to you before bed? Perhaps your mother reads to the family at breakfast? Your grandparents may enjoy reading books to you after school or on the weekends. You and your family members can create a Read-Together Chart and fill it in to keep track of all the books you've read together.

Here are two Read-Together Charts. The first one is a sample. The second one has been left blank, so you can add your own categories and books.

Sample Chart

Book We Read	Who Read It?	Summary	Our Review
The Secret Garden	My older sister read it to me.	It's about a spoiled girl who learns to love nature and people.	We like this book. The characters are funny, and the illustrations are beautiful!

Your Chart

This page may be reproduced as many times as needed.

96

Journal Topics

Choose one of these journal topics each day. Make sure you add enough detail so someone else reading this will clearly be able to know at least four of the following:

| ○ who | ○ what | ○ when | ○ where | ○ why | ○ how |

1. The perfect activity to do in the summer is . . .
2. Something amazing that I have seen is . . .
3. When I grow up, I want to be . . .
4. An animal that I would like to have as a pet is . . .
5. The last time I laughed really hard was . . .
6. A character from a movie that I really like is . . .
7. The best place to go on vacation is . . .
8. My room is . . .
9. A good friend is someone who . . .
10. When I am in the car for a long time, my favorite game to play is . . .
11. The best thing about technology is . . .
12. A famous person that I would like to meet is . . .
13. Whenever I am in a dark or confining space, I feel . . .
14. One dream I had lately was about . . .
15. During the weekend, I like to . . .
16. My family is made up of . . .
17. A book I enjoyed reading is . . .
18. When I am sad, I . . .
19. I usually forget to . . .
20. My favorite movie is . . .
21. If I won an award, it would be for . . .
22. If I could create another holiday, it would be for . . .
23. One habit I would really like to break is . . .
24. A food I like to eat is . . .
25. My favorite person to talk to is . . .

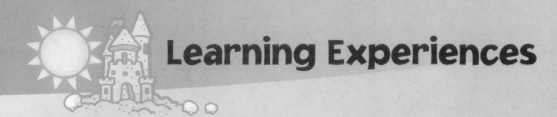

Learning Experiences

Here are some fun, low-cost activities that you can do with your child. You'll soon discover that these activities can be stimulating, educational, and complementary to the other exercises in this book.

Flash Cards

Make up all types of flash cards. Depending on your child's interest and grade level, these cards might feature enrichment words, math problems, or states and capitals. You can create them yourself with markers or on a computer. Let your child help cut pictures out of magazines and glue them on. Then, find a spot outdoors, and go through the flash cards with your child.

Project Pantry

Find a spot in your house where you can store supplies. This might be a closet or a bin that stays in one spot. Get some clean paint cans or buckets. Fill them with all types of craft and art supplies. Besides the typical paints, markers, paper, scissors, and glue, include some more unusual things, such as tiles, artificial flowers, and wrapping paper. This way, whenever you and your child want to do a craft project, you have everything you need at that moment.

The Local Library

Check out everything that your local library has to offer. Most libraries offer summer reading programs with various incentives. Spend an afternoon choosing and then reading books together.

Collect Something

Let your child choose something to collect that is free or inexpensive, such as paper clips or buttons. If your child wants to collect something that might be impractical, like horses, find pictures in magazines or catalogs, and have your child cut them out and start a picture collection.

Grocery Store Trip

Instead of making a trip to the grocery store a chore, make it a challenge. Even with nonreaders, you can have them help you find items on the shelf. Start by giving your child a list of his or her own. Review the list before you go. For nonreaders, you might want to cut pictures from ads. Many stores even have smaller shopping carts, so your child can have his or her own cart to fill. Once you get to an aisle where you know there is something on your child's list, prompt him or her to find the item. You may have to help your child get something down from a shelf.

Eating the Alphabet

Wouldn't it be fun to eat the alphabet? During the course of the summer, see how many fresh fruits and vegetables you can eat from A to Z. You and your child can make a poster or a chart with the letters A–Z on it. Once you have the chart, each time your child eats a fruit or vegetable, write it next to the matching letter of the alphabet. You can also let your child draw a picture of what he or she has eaten.

How Much Does It Cost?

If you go out for a meal, have your child help total the bill. Write down the cost of each person's meal. Then, have your child add them all together. You can vary this and make it much simpler by having your child just figure out the cost of an entrée and a drink or the cost of three desserts. You might want to round the figures first.

Nature Scavenger Hunt

Take a walk, go to a park, or hike in the mountains. But before you go, create a scavenger hunt list for your child. This can consist of all sorts of things found in nature. Make sure your child has a bag to carry everything he or she finds. (Be sure to check ahead of time about the rules or laws regarding removing anything.) You might include things like a leaf with pointed edges, a speckled rock, and a twig with two small limbs on it. Take a few minutes to look at all the things your child has collected, and check them off the list.

Measure It!

Using a ruler, tape measure, or yardstick is one way to see how tall something is. Start with your child, and find out how tall he or she is. Now find other things to measure and compare. Find out how much shorter a book is compared to your child, or discover how much taller the door is than your child. To measure things that can't be measured with a ruler, take some string and stretch it around the object. Cut or mark it where it ends. Then, stretch the string next to the ruler or tape measure to find out how long it is. Your child may be surprised at how different something that is the same number of inches looks when the shape is different.

Take a Trip, and Keep a Journal

If you are going away during the summer, have your child keep a journal. Depending on his or her age, this can take a different look. A young child can collect postcards and paste them into a blank journal. He or she can also draw pictures of places he or she is visiting. An older child can keep a traditional journal and draw pictures. Your child can also do a photo-journal if a camera is available for him or her to use.

Be a Scientist

Without your child's knowledge, put a ball inside a box, and cover it with a lid. Call in your child, and tell him or her to act like a scientist. He or she will need to ask questions and try to figure out answers like a scientist would. If your child is having a hard time asking questions, you may need to help. Some questions to ask include, "What do you think is inside the box?" and "How do you know?" Have your child shake the box and see if he or she can figure it out.

Web Sites

Math Web Sites

☼ **AAA Math:** http://www.aaamath.com
This site contains hundreds of pages of basic math skills divided by grade or topic.

☼ **AllMath.com:** http://www.allmath.com
This site has math flashcards, biographies of mathematicians, and a math glossary.

☼ **BrainBashers:** http://www.brainbashers.com
This is a unique collection of brainteasers, games, and optical illusions.

☼ **Coolmath.com:** http://www.coolmath.com
Explore this amusement park of mathematics! Have fun with the interactive activities.

☼ **Mrs. Glosser's Math Goodies:** http://www.mathgoodies.com
This is a free educational Web site featuring interactive worksheets, puzzles, and more!

Reading and Writing Web Sites

☼ **Aesop's Fables:** http://www.umass.edu/aesop
This site has almost forty of the fables. Both traditional and modern versions are presented.

☼ **American Library Association:** http://ala.org
Visit this site to find out both the past and present John Newbery Medal and Randolph Caldecott Medal winners.

☼ **Book Adventure:** http://www.bookadventure.com
This site features a free reading incentive program dedicated to encouraging children in grades K–8 to read.

☼ **Chateau Meddybemps—Young Writers Workshop:** http://www.meddybemps.com/9.700.html
Use the provided story starters to help your child write a story.

☼ **Fairy Godmother:** http://www.fairygodmother.com
This site will capture your child's imagination and spur it on to wonderful creativity.

☼ **Grammar Gorillas:** http://www.funbrain.com/grammar
Play grammar games on this site that proves that grammar can be fun!

☼ **Graphic Organizers:** http://www.eduplace.com/graphicorganizer
Use these graphic organizers to help your child write in an organized manner.

☼ **Rhymezone:** http://www.rhymezone.com
Type in the word you want to rhyme. If there is a rhyming word to match your word, you'll find it here.

☼ **Storybook:** http://www.kids-space.org/story/story.html
Storybook takes children's stories and publishes them on this Web site. Just like in a library, children can choose a shelf and read stories.

Web Sites (cont.)

Reading and Writing Web Sites (cont.)

☼ **Wacky Web Tales:** http://www.eduplace.com/tales/index.html

This is a great place for budding writers to submit their stories and read other children's writing.

☼ **Write on Reader:** http://library.thinkquest.org/J001156

Children can visit Write on Reader to gain a love of reading and writing.

General Web Sites

☼ **Animal Photos:** http://nationalzoo.si.edu

This site offers wonderful pictures of animals, as well as virtual zoo visits.

☼ **Animal Planet:** http://animal.discovery.com

Best for older kids, children can watch videos or play games at this site for animal lovers.

☼ **Congress for Kids:** http://www.congressforkids.net

Children can go to this site to learn all about the branches of the United States government.

☼ **Dinosaur Guide:** http://dsc.discovery.com/dinosaurs

This is an interactive site on dinosaurs that goes beyond just learning about the creatures.

☼ **The Dinosauria:** http://www.ucmp.berkeley.edu/diapsids/dinosaur.html

This site focuses on dispelling dinosaur myths. Read about fossils, history, and more.

☼ **Earthquake Legends:** http://www.fema.gov/kids/eqlegnd.htm

On this site, children can read some of the tales behind earthquakes that people of various cultures once believed.

☼ **The Electronic Zoo:** http://netvet.wustl.edu/e-zoo.htm

This site has links to thousands of animal sites covering every creature under the sun!

☼ **Great Buildings Online:** http://www.greatbuildings.com

This gateway to architecture around the world and across history documents a thousand buildings and hundreds of leading architects.

☼ **Maggie's Earth Adventures:** http://www.missmaggie.org

Join Maggie and her dog, Dude, on a wonderful Earth adventure.

☼ **Mr. Dowling's Electronic Passport:** http://www.mrdowling.com/index.html

This is an incredible history and geography site.

☼ **Sesame Street:** http://www.sesamestreet.org

There is no shortage of fun for children at Sesame Street.

☼ **Tropical Twisters:** http://kids.mtpe.hq.nasa.gov/archive/hurricane/index.html

Take an in-depth look at hurricanes, from how they're created to how dangerous they are.

Handwriting Chart

Aa Bb Cc Dd

Ee Ff Gg Hh

Ii Jj Kk Ll

Mm Nn Oo Pp

Qq Rr Ss Tt

Uu Vv Ww

Xx Yy Zz

Proofreading Marks

Editor's Mark	Meaning	Example
≡	capitalize	they fished in lake tahoe.
/	make it lowercase	Five Students missed the Bus.
sp.	spelling mistake	The day was clowdy and cold. _(sp.)_
⊙	add a period	Tomorrow is a holiday⊙
ℓ	delete (remove)	One person knew the the answer.
∧	add a word	Six ∧ were in the litter. _(pups)_
∧̣	add a comma	He planted peas ∧ corn, and squash.
∽	reverse words or letters	An otter swam in the bed kelp.
∨	add an apostrophe	The child's bike was blue.
∨ ∨	add quotation marks	Why can't I go? she cried.
#	make a space	He ate two red # apples.
⌒	close the space	Her favorite game is soft ball.
⁋	begin a new paragraph	to know. ⁋ Next on the list

Multiplication Chart

X	0	1	2	3	4	5	6	7	8	9
0	0	0	0	0	0	0	0	0	0	0
1	0	1	2	3	4	5	6	7	8	9
2	0	2	4	6	8	10	12	14	16	18
3	0	3	6	9	12	15	18	21	24	27
4	0	4	8	12	16	20	24	28	32	36
5	0	5	10	15	20	25	30	35	40	45
6	0	6	12	18	24	30	36	42	48	54
7	0	7	14	21	28	35	42	49	56	63
8	0	8	16	24	32	40	48	56	64	72
9	0	9	18	27	36	45	54	63	72	81

Measurement Tools

Measurement Conversion Chart

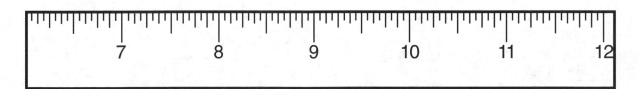 cups (c.)		1	2	4	8	16
pints (pt.)		$\frac{1}{2}$	1	2	4	8
quarts (qt.)		$\frac{1}{4}$	$\frac{1}{2}$	1	2	4
gallons (gal.)		$\frac{1}{16}$	$\frac{1}{8}$	$\frac{1}{4}$	$\frac{1}{2}$	1

Inch Ruler Cutout

Directions: Cut out the two ruler parts, and tape them together.

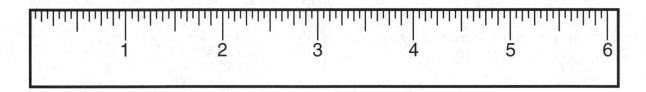

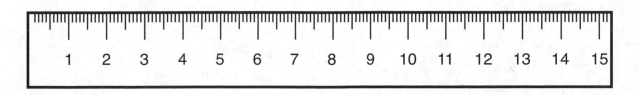

Centimeter Ruler Cutout

This page may be reproduced as many times as needed.

Answer Key

Page 11

Hidden word: HE

Page 12

3. not happy
4. is not able
5. not like
6. don't agree
7. not believable
8. before the test
9. before school
10. don't like

Page 13

1. 778
2. 406
3. 233
4. 491
5. 247
6. 700 + 60 + 5
7. 500 + 50 + 7
8. 100 + 80 + 6
9. 900 + 10 + 4
10. 200 + 10 + 5
11. one hundred twenty-nine
12. three hundred sixty-five
13. seven hundred ninety
14. six hundred sixty-one
15. two hundred ninety-six

Page 14

1. I had my birthday on a **T**uesday in **D**ecember.
2. We will take a trip on a **M**onday in **J**une.
3. I saw a football game on a **F**riday in **O**ctober.
4. Our class went to see <u>**T**he **M**usic **M**an</u>.
5. We read <u>**A**rrow to the **S**un</u> to study Native Americans.
6. My favorite book is <u>**H**arry **P**otter and the **S**orcerer's **S**tone</u>.

Page 15

2. 254   two hundred fifty-four
3. 165   one hundred sixty-five
4. 523   five hundred twenty-three
5. 436   four hundred thirty-six
6. 312   three hundred twelve
7. 654   six hundred fifty-four
8. 125   one hundred twenty-five

Smallest number: 125

Largest number: 654

Page 16

1. Tracy packed her coat.
2. Tracy packed her socks.
3. Tracy packed her pajamas.
4. Tracy packed her journal.
5. Tracy fell asleep.

Page 17

Ones-place barrel: 1, 3, 4, 7, 8

Tens-place barrel: 10, 37, 41, 83, 99

Hundreds-place barrel: 142, 291, 296, 429, 629

Page 18

1. The cat <u>curled up</u> on the <u>cushion</u> and <u>cried</u>.
2. One Saturday, a <u>silly</u> <u>snake</u> <u>slithered</u> in the dirt.
3. <u>Two</u> <u>tiny</u> turtles walked to the city.
4. The cold <u>wind</u> <u>whipped</u> past the lake.
5. The rain <u>poured</u> down on the <u>pavement</u>.
6. The <u>bear</u> ate <u>berries</u> for <u>breakfast</u>.

Page 19

36 blocks

Page 20

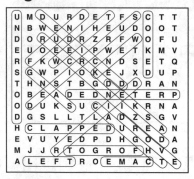

Page 21

Answer Key (cont.)

Page 22

2. "Line up at the door," said Mrs. Johnson.

3. Mom yelled, "Go, Cobras, go!"

4. Sheila wondered, "Should I wear my blue dress?"

5. My dad said, "You look nice today."

6. James asked, "May I have a glass of milk?"

7. "Please answer the phone," whispered my mother.

8. Kelly exclaimed, "Look out!"

9. "My lizard escaped," replied Henry sadly.

10. Juliette said, "I hope you can come over to play."

Page 23

1. 52	3. 80	5. 72
2. 70	4. 50	6. 35

Page 24

3. having a lot of wonder

4. having a lot of care

5. being happy

6. being soft

7. having a lot of color

8. having a lot of joy

9. being lonely

10. having a lot of harm

Page 25

2. 599	5. 903
3. 563	6. 890
4. 633	

Page 26

Answers will vary.

1. nibbled	6. stared
2. devoured	7. paced
3. stomped	8. gazed
4. gobbled	9. tiptoed
5. glanced	10. strolled

Page 27

One sample solution is noted below:

Row 1: **36, 38**, 31

Row 2: **37**, 33, **35**

Row 3: **32, 34**, 39

Page 28

1. She wore a red dress to school.

2. I can't wait for Christmas.

3. Shelly's new dog ate breakfast.

4. Daisies are pretty.

5. I wonder if I can go get pizza after the show.

Page 29

Top row: 84, 85, 83, 84

Bottom row: 83, 80, 87, 86, 81

Word: a crocodile

Page 30

Answers will vary.

Page 31

1. (+)912 or (–)648

2. (+)54 or (–)24

3. (+)1,339 or (–)525

4. (+)602 or (–)508

5. (+)400 or (–)224

6. (+)120 or (–)26

7. (+)2,901 or (–)2,707

8. (+)136 or (–)38

9. (+)1,197 or (–)89

Page 32

nose, nose, roll, hang, back, hognose

Page 33

2. $(32 − 4) + (49 − 7) = 70$

3. $(72 − 9) + (24 − 8) = 79$

4. $(56 − 7) + (64 − 8) = 105$

5. $(36 − 6) + (35 − 7) = 58$

Page 34

Answers will vary for 2–3. Possible meanings:

2. to fall; where a boat is kept

3. to repair; a problem

4. put up

5. get rid of someone from work

6. put clothes in a suitcase

Answer Key *(cont.)*

Page 35

1. 10	6. 31	11. 48
2. 1	7. 70	12. 20
3. 12	8. 33	13. 60
4. 50	9. 63	14. 21
5. 30	10. 11	15. 20

Page 36

1. They are sisters. They woke up in the same house and talked about "Mom."
2. They don't want to wake up Mom.
3. Answers may vary, but it is probably Mom's birthday.
4. She probably enjoys it.
5. It is probably some kind of gardening tool.

Page 37

1. 69	3. 35	5. 25
2. 18	4. 19	6. 11

Page 38

1. tripped
2. rides
3. ate
4. stood
5. scream
6. reads
7. slept
8. slipped
9. run
10. jumped

Page 39

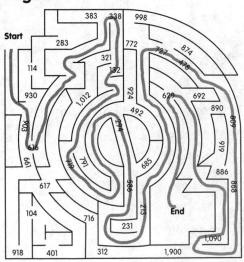

Page 40

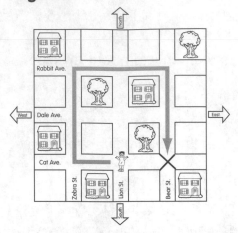

Page 41

1. 2 + 2 + 2 + 2 = 8
2. 4 x 2 = 8
3. 5 + 5 = 10
4. 2 x 5 = 10
5. 4 + 4 + 4 = 12
6. 3 x 4 = 12
7. 1 + 1 + 1 + 1 + 1 + 1 = 6
8. 6 x 1 = 6

Page 42

2. red—licorice
3. angry—man
4. interesting—story
5. long—letters
6–9. Answers will vary.

Page 43

X	0	1	2	3	4	5	6	7	8	9	10
0	0	0	0	0	0	0	0	0	0	0	0
1	0	1	2	3	4	5	6	7	8	9	10
2	0	2	4	6	8	10	12	14	16	18	20
3	0	3	6	9	12	15	18	21	24	27	30
4	0	4	8	12	16	20	24	28	32	36	40
5	0	5	10	15	20	25	30	35	40	45	50
6	0	6	12	18	24	30	36	42	48	54	60
7	0	7	14	21	28	35	42	49	56	63	70
8	0	8	16	24	32	40	48	56	64	72	80
9	0	9	18	27	36	45	54	63	72	81	90
10	0	10	20	30	40	50	60	70	80	90	100

Answer Key (cont.)

Page 44

2. pig-pen
3. snow-shoe
4. play-ground
5. clip-board
6. shoe-lace
7. bed-time
8. night-time
9. rain-bow
10. sun-shine

Page 45

1. 2	2. 14	3. 3	4. 1
5. 8	6. 12	7. 2	8. 2
9. 5	10. 12	11. 30	12. 16
13. 15			

Page 46

Answers will vary.

Page 47

1. 10
2. 5
3. 30
4. 55
5. 35
6. 50
7. 25
8. 50
9. 20
10. 45
11. 15
12. 40
13. 20
14. 55

Question: Can you multiply?

Page 48

Answers will vary.

Page 49

Dots: 4

Stripes: 3

Hearts: 6

Diamonds: 5

Squares: 2

1. hearts
2. squares
3. 20

Page 50

1. Cross off 80,121; 2,157; 7,418; 102.
2. Cross off 39,643; 29,253; 144,384.
3. Cross off 879; 579.
4. Cross off 66,175.
5. Cross off 9,780.
6. 805,457

Page 51

1. 4   2. 8   3. 4   4. 6   5. 7

Page 52

1. sh
2. ch
3. th
4. sh
5. th
6. sh
7. th
8. ch
9. wh

Page 53

1. 5, 5
2. 8, 8
3. 10, 10
4. 9, 9

Page 54

2. I like to play <u>soccer</u>, <u>golf</u>, and <u>tennis</u>.
3. I have <u>red</u>, <u>blue</u>, and <u>green</u> crayons.
4. I saw <u>lions</u>, <u>tigers</u>, and <u>bears</u> at the zoo.
5. Is this shape a <u>triangle</u>, <u>square</u>, or <u>circle</u>?
6. I practice on <u>Monday</u>, <u>Friday</u>, and <u>Sunday</u>.

Page 55

1. 12   2. 6   3. 10

Page 56

Answers will vary.

Answer Key *(cont.)*

Page 57
1. Each friend has 5 candies.
2. Each has 10 marbles.
3. Each friend has 3 flowers.

Page 58
Animals
A cat **meows**.
A duck **quacks**.
A dog **woofs**.
A sheep **baas**.
A horse **neighs**.
The Weather
The wind went **swoosh**.
The thunder **cracks**.
The rain goes **pitter-patter**.

Page 59
1. $3 \times 4 = 12$ or $4 + 4 + 4 = 12$
2. $2 \times 1 = 2$
3. $12 \div 3 = 4$
4. $5 \times 3 = 15$ or $5 + 5 + 5 = 15$
5. $5 \times 3 = 15$ or $3 + 3 + 3 + 3 + 3 = 15$
6. $25 \div 5 = 5$
7. $12 \div 2 = 6$
8. $10 \div 5 = 2$
9. $100 \div 10 = 10$

Page 60
Answers will vary.

Page 61
2. $\dfrac{4}{6}$ 3. $\dfrac{2}{5}$ 4. $\dfrac{3}{4}$ 5. $\dfrac{1}{2}$

6. $\dfrac{1}{2}$ 7. $\dfrac{5}{9}$ 8. $\dfrac{1}{4}$

Page 62
1. told us to stand, read us a story
2. barked at the cat, chewed the bone
3. built a nest in the tree, is singing a song
5–6. Sentences will vary.

Page 63
1. $\dfrac{6}{10}$ 2. $\dfrac{2}{10}$ 3. $\dfrac{5}{8}$ 4. $\dfrac{7}{8}$

5. $\dfrac{10}{12}$ 6. $\dfrac{10}{100}$ 7. $\dfrac{1}{2}$ 8. $\dfrac{20}{100}$

9. $\dfrac{1}{10}$, $\dfrac{1}{4}$, $\dfrac{1}{3}$

10. $\dfrac{3}{10}$, $\dfrac{5}{10}$, $\dfrac{8}{10}$

11. $\dfrac{2}{5}$, $\dfrac{2}{4}$, $\dfrac{2}{3}$

12. $\dfrac{1}{8}$, $\dfrac{3}{8}$, $\dfrac{7}{8}$

13. $1\dfrac{1}{2}$, 2, $4\dfrac{1}{2}$

14. $\dfrac{1}{6}$, $\dfrac{1}{5}$, $\dfrac{1}{2}$

Page 64
1. buddies, friends
2. baby, infant
3. quietly, silently
4. shop, store
5. gift, present
6. attractive, handsome

Page 65
1. $\dfrac{2}{4}$ 2. $\dfrac{3}{6}$ 3. $\dfrac{2}{3}$ 4. $\dfrac{2}{5}$

5. $\dfrac{4}{6}$ 6. $\dfrac{5}{10}$ 7. $\dfrac{4}{10}$ 8. $\dfrac{4}{8}$

9. $\dfrac{1}{3}$ 10. $\dfrac{3}{5}$ 11. $\dfrac{2}{5}$ 12. $\dfrac{2}{3}$

Page 66
2. underline   5. circle
3. circle   6. underline
4. underline   7. underline
Sentences will vary.

Answer Key (cont.)

Page 67

1. cookie
2. pie
3. ◐ or ⊖
4. ⊞ or ⊠
5. ▤ or ⫼

Page 68

Answers will vary.

Page 69

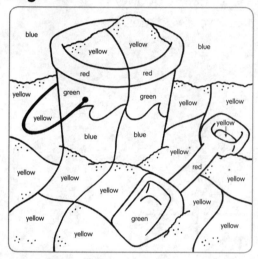

Page 70

1. apple
2. basket
3. cat
4. eagle
5. elephant
6. house
7. school
8. shoe
9. yo-yo
10. zebra

Page 71

1. 6 marbles
2. 19 − 8 = 11 footballs
3. 9 + 7 + 5 + 3 + 7 = 31 points
4. 21 ÷ 7 = 3 tennis balls

Page 72

1. down
2. dry
3. go
4. awake
5. day
6. solid

Page 73

1. 16 + 27 = 43
2. 28 + 46 = 74
3. $53.00 − $28.00 = $25.00
4. 83 − 65 = 18

Page 74

1. hard
2. quickly
3. intently
4. fast
5. slowly
6. loudly

7–10. Answers will vary.

Page 75

1. 367 marbles
2. 125 candies
3. 3 dollar bills
4. $9.49

Page 76

1. a
2. a
3. c
4. c

Page 77

2. 4 more monkeys in the tree
3. 45 cups
4. 267 books
5. 24 pencils
6. 4 flowers

Page 78

Answers will vary.

Page 79

G	B	Y	O	R	P
O	R	P	B	Y	G
R	P	G	Y	B	O
B	Y	O	P	G	R
Y	O	R	G	P	B
P	G	B	R	O	Y

Answer Key (cont.)

Page 80

```
M A I L B O X
      U             G
   N  T          R  R
   E  T       R  A  A
   W  E       A  N  S
   S  R       I  D  S
D  P  F       N  M  H
O  A  T A B L E C L O T H
O  P  Y       O  T  P
R  E          A  H  P
C U P B O A R D   E  E
E  L          T   R  R
L  L                
L          L I P S T I C K
```

Page 81

2. 150 + 130 + 210 = 490; Mariah bought 490 party items in all.

3. 190 − 90 = 100; 100 people said "no."

4. 210 + 320 + 60 = 590; Lucy set out 590 jellybeans.

5. 570 − 240 = 330 − 200 = 130; The third cupcake had 130 sprinkles.

6. 220 + 300 + 370 = 890; 890 points were scored in all.

Page 82
Answers will vary.

Page 83
Estimates will vary.

1. $2.96
2. $1.53
3. $2.62
4. $6.04
5. $2.44

Page 84

1. noise
2. loud
3. crowd
4. town
5. cowboys
6. newspaper
7. Roy
8. boy
9. grew
10. choice

Page 85

1. 2
2. 2
3. 3
4. 4

Page 86
Answers will vary.

Page 87

1. 2 pennies, 2 dimes, 1 quarter
2. 3 quarters
3. 1 penny, 1 nickel, 1 dime, 1 quarter
4. 2 half dollars
5. 2 nickels, 2 dimes, 2 quarters
6. 1 penny, 2 nickels, 4 dimes

Page 88

1. 9:00 a.m.
2. 20
3. Art
4. Mr. Castle
5. 10:45 a.m.
6. Quiet reading time

Page 89

O	G	Y	R	P	B
R	P	B	G	Y	O
P	B	R	O	G	Y
G	Y	O	B	R	P
Y	O	G	P	B	R
B	R	P	Y	O	G

Page 90

Row 1 Across: chocolate syrup on left scoop

Row 2 Across: chocolate sprinkles

Row 3 Across: chocolate chips

Row 1 Down: drip

Row 2 Down: white spoons

Row 3 Down: black spoons

Diagonal (from top left down): black-bottom bowls

Diagonal (from top right down): two cherries